Religious Thought of Modern India

Nakka Krupanandam, M.A., B.L., Ph.D., is a development activist. He is presently the Project Officer for Konaseema Animation Programme, run by the Social Service Centre, Eluru, for the welfare of tsunami victims. Also he is the National Secretary of Society of St. Vincent De Paul, National Council of India, Mumbai, and Honorary Chairman, Home for the Aged, Nirmalagiri, Andhra Pradesh.

Religious Thought of Modern India

With Special Reference to Raja Rammohun Roy, Swami Vivekananda, Mahatma Gandhi and Dr. S. Radhakrishnan

N. Krupanandam

Readworthy
New Delhi

First published 2010

Readworthy Publications (P) Ltd.

Editorial & Regd. Office
A-18, Mohan Garden
Near Nawada Metro Station
New Delhi–110 059-06
Phone: 011-2537 1324
Fax: +91-11-2537 1323

Sales Office
4735/22, Prakash Deep Building,
Ground Floor, Ansari Road, Daryaganj
New Delhi–110 002-02
Phone: 011-43549197
Fax: +91-11-23243060

Email: info@readworthypub.com
Web: www.readworthypub.com

Cataloging in Publication Data--DK

Courtesy: D.K. Agencies (P) Ltd. <docinfo@dkagencies.com>

Krupanandam, N. (Nakka)

Religious thought of modern India: with special reference to Raja Rammohun Roy, Swami Vivekananda, Mahatma Gandhi and Dr. S. Radhakrishnan / N. Krupanandam.

p. cm.

Includes bibliographical references (p.) and index.

ISBN 13: 978-93-5018-008-2 ISBN 10: 93-5018-008-1

1. Religion--Philosophy. 2. Hindu philosophy. 3. Rammohun Roy, Raja, 1772?-1833. 4. Vivekananda, Swami, 1863-1902. 5. Gandhi, Mahatma, 1869-1948. 6. Radhakrishnan, S. (Sarvepalli), 1888-1975. I. Title.

DDC 210.1 22

Printed at Salasar Imaging Systems, Delhi-35

I dedicate this book to my beloved parents Shri N. Venkanna and Late Mrs. N. Bhagyavathi for giving me this life, leading me in religious and spiritual matters, teaching me to perceive what is good and what is bad, and making me what I am today.

Key to Transliteration

Vowels and Diphthongs

अ	a	उ	u	ए	e
आ	ā	ऊ	ū	ऐ	ai
इ	i	ऋ	ṛ	ओ	o
ई	ī	ॠ	ṝ	ऑ	ô
		ऌ	ḷ	औ	au

Consonants

Gutturals		Palatals		Cerebrals		Dentals	
क	ka	च	ca	ट	ṭa	त	ta
ख	kha	छ	cha	ठ	ṭha	थ	tha
ग	ga	ज	ja	ड	ḍa	द	da
घ	gha	झ	jha	ड़	ṛa	ध	dha
ङ	ṅa	ञ	ña	ढ	ḍha	न	na
				ढ़	ṛha		
				ण	ṇa		

Labials		Semivowels		Sibilants		Aspirate	
प	pa	य	ya	श	śa	ह	ha
फ	pha	र	ra	ष	ṣa		
ब	ba	ल	la	स	sa		
भ	bha	व	va				
म	ma						

Conjunct Characters

क्ष	kṣa	ज्ञ	jña	and others similarly

Anusvāra		Anunāsika		Visarga		Avagraha	
ं	ṃ	ँ	ṅ, m̐	:	ḥ	ऽ	'(apostrophe)

Preface

There have been many works on Indian philosophy from the view point of various Indian philosophers—ancient and modern. Philosophy is to question the religious beliefs and practices. My work undertakes an analysis of the trends in the philosophies of four thinkers, namely, Raja Rammohun Roy, Swami Vivekananda, Mahatma Gandhi and Dr. S. Radhakrishanan. Renaissance occurred during the 19th century and the modern philosophy began. In this book I have presented the views of the four thinkers where I have analyzed their philosophies. This book brings out the commonalities in the philosophies of the above four thinkers. All of them were influenced by their contemporary social setup and their philosophies emerged as the answers to the problems prevalent in those days. They all believed in *karma, bhakti, jnana* and *yoga*. Each one of them stressed and believed in any one of these four margas.

Raja Rammohun Roy stressed *jnana*, Swami Vivekananda stressed *karma*, Mahatma Gandhi stressed *bhakti* and Dr. S. Radhakrishnan stressed *jnana*. This book brings out the common trends in the four thinkers who were true to Indian tradition but reverent to other traditions too. The highest aim of any individual of any religion should be the attainment of Moksha. The essence of ancient Indian religious thought is individual salvation and it is based on meditative speculation. It is purely salvation orientation. But the essence of modern Indian religious thought is group salvation, i.e. salvation of the humanity.

Modern religious thought is based on experience and it blends spirituality and materialism. We see that modern thinkers taking the help of psychology to understand some of the complex philosophical concepts like soul. All the above modern thinkers are influenced by the Christianity, the Islam and the Marxism.

This book also discusses the secularism and tries to find an answer to the question of truth and religion. It deals with the intellect and intuition. Intuition is a basis of religion and is source of all knowledge. But some philosophers like our former Prime Minister Jawaharlal Nehru and M. N. Roy tried to limit the role of religion in the modern trends. But Raja Rammohun Roy believes that religion is the background of science which explains and explores nature which is the essence of religion. This book discusses the concepts of theism and atheism in reference to truth. All the thinkers conclude that if people are scientific and rational in temperament they should reject many tenets in many religions which seem to be irrational. But modern man is scientific in temperament but coming to religion faith dominates region and rationality.

Modern thinkers give equal importance to four *Purusharthas*, namely, *dharma*, *artha*, *kama* and *moksha*. They give equal importance to spiritual life as well as material worldly life. They believe in one God whose names may differ. All of them conclude that man cannot shape his own destiny without the intervention of God.

I hope my work should influence you and your thinking and help you understand the essence of life. I would like to present the religious tolerance and the religious harmony as the answer to all the problems existing in the world today. The contemporary world is full of evil today as people lack the real understanding of the essence of their religion. I hope all the violence in this world is erased and it is replaced by humanity which is based on love and service, the essence of all religions.

Acknowledgements

My grateful thanks are due to Dr. S.C. Suguna Kumari, Associate Professor, Department of Philosophy and Religious Studies, Andhra University, for her able guidance and valuable suggestions at various stages of drafting of this book. I wish to thank Prof. M.V. Krishnayya, former Head of the Department of Philosophy and Religious Studies, Andhra University, for his kind suggestions.

I am grateful to Prof. L. Venugopal Reddy, Vice Chancellor, Andhra University, and Prof. P. Vijaya Prakash, Registrar, Andhra University, for their help and good wishes.

I am thankful to Prof. J.V. Prabhakara Rao, Principal, College of Arts and Commerce, for the encouragement he gave in the completion of this book.

My thanks are due to Prof. T. Christanandam, Head of the Department of Philosophy and Religious Studies, for his kind co-operation and valuable suggestions for the completion of this work.

I am also immensely thankful to my teacher Prof. P. George Victor, Chairman, Board of Studies, Department of Philosophy and Religious Studies, for his encouragement and help.

I offer my heartfelt thanks and deep sense of gratitude to Prof. G. Veerraju, Prof. G.V. Raju (Retired), Prof. S.D.A. Joga Rao and Sri. B. Ravi Babu, Asst. Professor, for their valuable suggestions and help.

My thanks are also due to Prof. S. Satyanarayana, Prof. Y.V. Satyanarayana, Prof. V.V.S. Saibaba, Dr. (Mrs.) K.R. Rajani, Associate Professor, and Dr. B.V.S. Bhanusree, Associate Professor, Department of Philosophy and Religious Studies.

I would like to express my gratitude to Mr. V. Anji Babu and Mr. Srinivas Rao.

I would like to express my thanks to Prof. C. Sasikala, Librarian, Dr. V.S. Krishna and her supporting staff. I am grateful to Mr. B. Prasada Rao, Librarian, School of Distance Education, Andhra University, Mr. N.V. Prasada Rao, Librarian, A.U. Study Centre, School of Distance Education, Sir. C.R.R. College campus, Eluru, for their encouragement and cooperation. My special thanks are due to Mr. M. Joseph, for his help.

I am extremely grateful and deeply indebted to Bishop John Mulagada, Bishiop of Eluru, Fr. P. Bala, Fr. G. Moses, Fr. Rayappa, Fr. Maria Joji, Fr. Y. Marriddy, Fr. G.J. Charles, Fr. N.J.M. Kumar, Mother Mirium, Adoration Monastery and all the Sisters for their valuable prayers for all the time for me and for my family. My sincere thanks to Mr. Pagano and my sister Mrs. D. Jayakumari.

I cannot adequately express my gratitude to Mr. B. Suvarna Kumar, my bosom friend and brother and his wife Mrs. B. Young Hanna for rendering valuable guidance and prayers. My special thanks to my brothers and all the family members and also to my father-in-law and mother-in-law and loving thanks to my brother-in-law Mr. Y. Govardhan Paratpara Rao and my sister Mrs. Y. Saroja Govardhan for their help rendered to my wife and children during the period of my absence.

My deepest thanks are due to my beloved wife Mrs. N. Vijaya Lakshmi who has been a constant source of inspiration to me. I am indebted to her, without whose constant support I would not have completed my work. I love my children Vijyothi, Vimal Clare and Vijay Anthony for their joyful presence while doing this work.

I would like to express my deep felt thanks to Mr. D. Abraham, Executive Director, APSSS, Mr. V.M.J. Balaswamy, National President, National Council of India, SSVP, Mr. P. Charles, Mr. K. Verrabbai and Mr. Peddi Raju for their constant support to me in my work.

Contents

1

Introduction

In the history of Indian philosophical and religious tradition, the 19th century has a great significance. During this period, the Indian religious thought was greatly influenced by the Western tradition. In Indian tradition and ethos, religion plays an important role. The period ending about four and half centuries before 1945 was a period of Western dominance. As Toynbee remarks, "During these 450 years the West was an aggressor on the whole and the world was hit hard by the West."[1] The intrusion of the West began when Vasco Da Gama found the sea route to India in 1498. The process of decolonization set with the withdrawal of British forces from India in 1947 and the European Navy from China in 1949. This period (1498 to 1945) constitutes "a clearly marked epoch of history" presenting a singular unity in its fundamental aspects. The European powers, mainly the English, the French, the Portuguese and the Dutch, wanted to conquer India but finally the English were successful in this attempt.

In a broader sense, whether the English or the French, it is Europeans that matter in spite of different languages and civilizations. During the period (1498 to 1945), the European civilization was far advanced in almost all spheres of human endeavour. In science, technology, arts and literature, power and administration, they were the masters of the globe. Asia, Africa and Latin America were less advanced, and they had to learn a lot from the European civilization. The process of

1 K. Satchidananda Murthy, *Indian philosophy since 1498*, p.1.

modernization began in the West. The French Revolution and industrial revolution were the proximate causes for the modernization of the West.

The French Revolution had greater impact across the world. As Condorcet said, its principles were purer, more precise and deeper than those that guided the Americans. The framework of ideas provided by the French Revolution was abstract enough to become universal. The industrial revolution created new material conditions of human existence, i.e. a new manner and method of producing means of subsistence and exchanging and consuming the products so produced. As the material mode of existence is a major determining element in history, this revolution caused a re-structuring of the society. The social process of modernization setting motion by the industrial revolution made the West dynamic, expansive and aggressive.

Impact of Modernization

Many nations of the Eastern world deliberately began to imitate the West by adopting wholesale, the technology that arose in the industrialized West, along with all the ideas and institutions which were inseparable from it. It was found that the technology was an indivisible part of a new way of life, a new civilization, and unless the people lived this life, they could not master this technology.

The choice that confronted the Western world was between industrialization and adoption of Western institutions. The first man to realize this was the Russian Czar Peter the Great (1682 AD-1725). Within two centuries, Russia caught with the West by adopting Western technology and ideas. In Japan, everything was modernized (Ishin); and it became a unified, industrialized and modern state and a world power. Similarly, Turkey became a modern nation under the leadership of Mustafa Kemal Pasha.[2]

2 K. Satchidananda Murthy, *Indian philosophy since* 1498, p.24.

In India, when the East India Company began to rule it also wanted to bring changes in education and administration to make India a modern state. The administration of Marquees Wellesley (1798–1805) marks the definite beginning of the modern period in Indian history. To consolidate their empire and develop their resources in India with a view to appropriate them, but incidentally to promote welfare of India, the British had to introduce machinery like railways, telegraphs and press, undertake irrigation projects, give people English education and raise a modern Indian Army. All these steps set a motion to the process of industrialization and urbanization. While the process of modernization began in Russia, Japan and Turkey was initiated by their rulers, in India it was imposed by the British.[3]

The Europeans were not at all of equal culture. Some of the Asian colonies had a long and hoary history of civilization and culture. While they were prepared to accept the advantages of Western technology, they were not prepared to forego their civilization and culture. The early rulers wanted to spread the European educational system and also considered that preaching of Christianity was beneficial to the natives of these countries. This approach had given good results to colonial powers in Africa and Latin America. In some of these countries, the people were not having a literary tradition and some of them did not have even a script for their languages. In accepting Western civilization and its value system, we find that some of these countries had accepted the technology liberally; but at the same time, they were not completely westernized.

India is an example which has taken all that is good and useful from Western civilization and, at the same time, retaining its cultural ethos. The contemporary Indian thinkers who influenced Indian culture are Raja Rammohun Roy, Keshab Chandra Sen, Ramakrishna Paramahamsa, Swami Vivekananda, Dayananda Saraswati, Balagangadhar Tilak,

---

3 K. Satchidananda Murthy, *Indian philosophy since 1498*, p.25.

Sri Narayana Guru, Rabindranath Tagore, Mahatma Gandhi, Aurobindo Ghose, Sarvepalli Radhakrishnan and Jiddu Krishnamurthy—to name a few.

Except Sri Ramakrishna Paramahamsa and Dayananda Saraswati—all others were influenced by Western education and culture. Their appreciation of Western value system did not come in their way of nationalism and patriotism. All these thinkers are generally considered as modern Indian thinkers. Many of them had taken *Vedānta* as the main plank on which they wanted to build their philosophies and social thought. All of them were for reform, social change and modernization. But we find some divergence in their views regarding the methods and process of social transformation.

Contemporary Indian Thought

Generally the philosophical thought of eighteenth and nineteenth centuries onwards, i.e. after the advent of British in India, is considered as contemporary or modern Indian thought. Contemporary Indian thinkers try to reinterpret some of the ancient ideas derived mainly from the *Vedānta*. In their philosophy, one could find refreshingly new ideas. For many of them, *Vedānta* is the base on which a new way of life and a new world order can be built.

The contemporary Indian thinkers acknowledge the reality of suffering and speak about the possibility of an escape from it. They consider that life has meaning and purpose and it helps us in the process of spiritual growth. They believe that the ideal of life can be reached only by transcending this finite world. All of them assert that to be in this world is not a misfortune. Indian philosophy today is at the cross-roads. "It is anxious to retain the forces of the centuries of its' tradition through which it has grown, and yet it cannot afford to overlook the 'scientific facts' and 'the empirical attitude' of the present-day world."[4]

4 B.K. Lal, *Contemporary Indian philosophy*, p. XV.

It is in such a state of inner conflict that the contemporary Indian thinker develops his system of thought. He tries to escape this predicament by asserting the value of the essentials of tradition with a renewed vigour emphasizing that these essentials are not against the scientific temper of the present-day world. Consequently, what they have been able to evolve is some kind of an East-West synthesis.

Every country, which has a tradition of philosophic speculation, has its own approach. For example, it is said that the British philosophy is generally empirical. American philosophy is considered as realistic and pragmatic. French philosophy is mainly rationalistic, while German philosophy is pre-eminently speculative. In the same vein, Indian philosophy can be described as meditative.

> The Indian Philosopher is not just a romantic. He is much more than that. He is able to meditate upon the extraordinary powers of both nature and man. "Philosophy in India invariably arises in some such acts of meditative speculation. It was so with the *Vedic* seer and also with the *Upaniṣadic* thinker and it continues to be so even with the contemporary Indian thinker. Just as experience provides the backbone of every kind of British philosophy, so meditative speculation has been the method of the Indian philosopher throughout history."[5]

Life, according to ancient Indian philosophy, is full of suffering. The aim of religion and philosophy is to attain freedom from suffering. The contemporary Indian thinker accepts this reality of suffering and speaks about the possibility of an escape from it. Some of the thinkers like Tagore and Radhakrishnan consider the existential conditions of man, and speak of the life of care and anguish—of fear and boredom—and assert that life means living in the midst of people in spite of

5 B.K. Lal, *Contemporary Indian philosophy*, p. XII.

them. Philosophy is concerned with the existential individual living in the midst of his life situation; but the ultimate ideal is the redemption of both the individual and the community.

The ancient Indian thinkers gave importance to the control of the body, senses and mind for the spiritual growth of the individual. They consider that senses and the mind are not to be subdued but sublimated. The world is considered as the only field for action and the body as the temple of the divine. They give importance to body and senses in the process of spiritual growth. In this aspect the contemporary Indian thinkers consider themselves to be close to empirical and the 'matter-of-fact' of the present times.

The ancient Indian philosophers believed that suffering was on account of our ignorance regarding the nature of the real. When we cannot make a distinction between the real and the unreal, we wrongly develop an attachment for the unreal and the transient and thus suffer. But the contemporary Indian thinkers view the problem in a different way. They believe that philosophy is an attitude—a way of looking at things. Even if the life situation remains the same, a person who has proper perspective can adopt and solve the issues.

The contemporary Indian thinkers have not come out of the old tradition. The concepts of *karma,* rebirth, salvation, etc. are the same issues on which they show interest. But their approach to these issues is different. The development of sciences, both natural and social, has given us new dimensions to our approach to solve these issues. These thinkers feel that these problems do not change but they can be viewed from different perspective. The contemporary Indian thinkers, taking the advantage of their knowledge of the sciences, try to look at these problems from different angles. Sciences like sociology, anthropology and psychology can give us new approach to solve some of the philosophical problems.

There are some prominent issues regarding which all these thinkers appear to be in agreement. They have belief in a god reality of the world, integral nature of man, reality of human freedom and the importance of reason and revelation. All of them are monists but with different approaches. Similarly, all of them give importance to human dignity. For them, being born as a human being is not a misfortune but a great blessing. It is through human life one can attain freedom or liberation.

All of them have recognized the importance of reason and intuition. Thus they have accepted the necessity of both rationalism and empiricism. They believe that reality can be known only through some intuitive awareness and everybody is capable of having some intuitive awareness and by constant practice one is able to intensify the powers inherent in mind. Man can have intuitive cognitions of the reality. These thinkers assert that this is not a mysterious faculty. It is natural to man and is inherently present in every individual. They have similar notions regarding human freedom. It is not simply ethical or social; it is metaphysical and existential, and they believed that man is free, both existentially and metaphysically. Though man is potentially free, certain obstacles come in his way. But he can overcome them to get full freedom.

The contemporary Indian thinkers give importance to life in this world and assert that even after realizing *mokṣa* the work of individual is not over. He has to live in the world, trying to help those in need. Thus a liberated man has a social obligation to help other fellowmen in their upliftment.

The modern society gives importance to welfare of the individual and the society. Almost all religions give importance to social well-being.

All major religions like Christianity, Islam and Hinduism in the pre-modern days gave importance to individual's moral behaviour and spiritual development. They did not give importance to worldly well-being and social well-being. But contemporary thoughts, both in the East and the West, give importance to the worldly life and well-being of the individual and the community.

In contemporary philosophy, the other problem is related to the variation in academic and the actual philosophies. Academic philosophy, based on high speculation and reasoning, develops philosophical systems and some of them are not applicable to society. There are other thinkers who give importance to day-to-day life and thus missing the high academic and intellectual excellence. Only few thinkers like Swami Vivekananda and Mahatma Gandhi wanted that their ideas should be put into practice. That is why, both the common men and the scholars derive satisfaction from their writings.

In the West, philosophy has become highly technical and the exclusive pursuit of some academic men, confined only to some universities. For them, philosophy, broadly speaking, is a style of thinking, a way of reflection with the help of which muddles, ambiguities, vagueness, etc. can be cleared, new insights can be gained and new issues can be raised. For them, philosophy is purely an intellectual pursuit for the joy of it, and at best for the clarification of concepts. The contemporary Indian thinkers, while conceding the positive claims of their Western counterparts, are not prepared to agree with them in their negative assertions. That is why, in their writings one comes across both scholarly and highly intellectual analysis and deliberations and also positive suggestions regarding conduct, behaviour and the way of life.

All the contemporary thinkers are humanists and some of them combine both humanism and humanitarianism. For example, Swami Vivekananda's approach is humanistic but at the same time he recommends very strongly humanitarian work and service. Humanism these days has come to acquire a definite import. It says that man can shape his own destiny. The development in science and technology and ever increasing capacity of mankind in controlling the forces of nature have given man a sort of self confidence. Man began to assert that he can shape his own destiny and that he need not rely upon any supernatural or spiritual powers. This kind of humanism is positivistic, secular and worldly in outlook.

There is some conflict between scientific humanism and the humanism supported by these thinkers. The contemporary Indian thinkers have an unflinching faith in the ultimacy of spiritual pursuits and ideals. They have obliterated the opposition between humanism and spiritualism. They assert that human aspirations are ever increasing and man is not satisfied with what he has achieved.

Man always tries to achieve something more than what he has. The normal desires have to be given their due. But there is something more than these normal desires. Spiritualism is nothing but trying to satisfy those urges of man that transcend the normal physical level. As B.K. Lal remarks, "If humanism is allowed full expression, both the kinds of aspirations will have to be satisfied. In that sense, spiritualism no longer remains incompatible with humanism, but becomes an aspect of it. It is in this sense that contemporary Indian philosophy, in spite of its emphasis on spiritual ideals, is humanistic."[6]

Four major thinkers of 19th and 20th centuries are taken up in this study. They are: Raja Rammohun Roy (1772–1833), Swami Vivekananda (1863–1902), Mahatma Gandhi (1869-1948) and Dr. Sarvepalli Radhakrishnan (1888–1975).

All these thinkers were eminent leaders and they had contributed substantially towords the religious, social and political development of Indian society. After the advent of British rule in India, the whole administrative system had changed gradually. The English language was slowly introduced as the medium of instruction. With the introduction

6 B.K. Lal, *Contemporary Indian philosophy*, p. XXI.

of English, the vast literature, as well as science and technology of the West began to influence the Indian society. The *Pāṭhaśālā* system of the Hindus and *Madrasā* system of the Muslims taught only religious scriptures and some earlier literature in those languages. Thus the knowledge imparted was religious and limited. With the introduction of English, all the modern sciences and arts were begun to be taught; and the universities (Calcutta, Bombay and Madras) were started in 1857.

Though there was some suspicion in the beginning about the new system of education, people and leaders gradually realized the importance and benefit of the new system of education. This education made the students exposed to all the knowledge available in arts, science and technology. All the best literature of Europe (European languages) was translated into English and through English all this knowledge became available to the Indian students. Though the main aim of Macaulay in introducing English was to get enough persons to serve the East India Company, the results were altogether different. English education made the Indian society step into modernization. This process had its effect on all aspects of Indian life.

We will find that the thinkers, about whom we are discussing, were the products of English education. The impact of this system of education made these thinkers constructive and reformative in their approach. All these leaders were highly educated, brilliant and prolific in their writings.

Raja Rammohun Roy

More has been written about Raja Rammohun Roy than about any other Indian who lived during the first half of the 19th century. His contributions to Indian culture are so substantial. He set precedents in many of his activities. He was one of the first Indians to establish his own press and published pamphlets and books as well as regular newspapers.

> "He was the first and the most prominent Indian to become involved in the campaign for the abolition of *Satī* (the concremation of widows). He was in the early years of 19th century the most articulate Indian to protest against British administrative injustices."[7]

He was one of the most active proponents of universal education system, which would incorporate both Indian and European knowledge. He was also responsible for getting traditional religious texts translated, printed and distributed to the public. Rammohun set many precedents which were later followed by many political, social and religious reformers. He faced much criticism from his contemporaries. They criticized him, and accused him as being a Christian or an atheist. They accused him of attempting to destroy the Hindu tradition. Some accused him that he was trying to undermine all religious traditions. Rammohun's religious thought has been summarized in numerous books, articles and public addresses. But there has been very little systematic analysis of his religious thought. Since his death in England in 1833, most discussions of his life have been descriptive and adulatory. Only in recent years we have some analyses of his religious thought.[8]

The broad outlines of Rammohun Roy's religious activities are well known. He opposed polytheism and idol worship. He supported ethical monotheism. He challenged the theological adequacy of Trinitarian Christianity. In his later days, he established the *Brahmo Samāj* as a place of worship, with the help of those who shared his religious convictions. Rammohun in his book *Tuhfatul* criticized religious leaders. He maintained that the canons of reason demanded universality and freedom from contradiction of all religious statements.

---

7 Raja Rammohun Roy's most famous protests were against the Press Ordinance of March 14, 1823 (C. *Collect life and letters*) pp. 423-54.

8 Ajit Kumar Roy, *The religious ideas of Rammohun Roy*, pp. 71-91.

What distinguishes Raja Rammohun Roy's thought from his predecessors was his insistence that religious traditions must be evaluated by external rather than internal criteria. True authority, according to him, did not depend upon adherence to dietary regulations, avoidance of foreigners, position, birth or personal claim to revelation. The basis for authority was knowledge and morality. Institutional religious leaders had legitimate authority only to the extent that they were moral and knowledgeable.

Raja Rammohun Roy established *Brahmo Samāj* in 1828 and inaugurated a form of worship consistent with these assumptions. The worship was congregational and the service consisted of readings from the *Upaniṣads, Brahma Sūtra* and *Vedas*, and exposition of these readings with prayer and singing. In the worship services, there were no prohibitions against the attendance of any person of any caste, religion or nationality.[9]

K.C. Mitra referred to Raja Rammohun Roy as a 'Religious Benthamite.'[10] He seemed to mean that Raja Rammohun Roy evaluated religious beliefs and practices largely on the basis of their utility. His concern for the social implications of religious doctrines contributed significantly to his interest in the teachings of Jesus. In the introduction to his book, *The Precepts of Jesus*, Roy says: "The simple code of religion and morality is admirable, calculated to elevate men's ideas to high and liberal notions of God... and is so well fitted to regulate the conduct of human race in the discharge of their various duties to themselves and to society, that I cannot but hope the best effects from the promulgation in the present form."[11] There seems to be ample evidence to support a growing number of

---

9 For a description of the establishment of Brahmo Samaj, see *Brahmo Samaj and the making of modern India* by David Kopf. pp. 209-50.

10 Kishore Chandra Mitra, Raja Rammohun Roy, *Calcutta Review*, 4th July-December, 1845; p. 388.

11 *Swami Vivekananda's works*, 5; 4.

scholars, who have recently interpreted Raja Rammohun Roy primarily as a religious utilitarian whose central concern was the wellbeing of society. Raja Rammohun Roy's social concern signaled change from an emphasis on mystery and metaphysics to ethics and philanthropy.[12] This change of emphasis which Roy's work expresses so clearly is characteristic of substantial amount of 19th century Indian thought. Theology and metaphysics became tools of ethics and social change.[13]

Swami Vivekananda

Swami Vivekananda is considered as the harbinger of modern Indian Renaissance. He was a voracious reader. During his college days he read the works of Hume, Herbert Spencer and John Stuart Mill. *Brahmo Samāj* was spreading its ideas in Bengal at that time. Many of the middle class Hindus and the elite of Bengal were influenced by the ideals of *Brahmo Samāj*. The impact of Western civilization and the Christian culture was engulfing Bengal. The aim of *Brahmo Samāj* was to reform the Hinduism and to stop the impact of Western culture and Christianity. The Christian teachings appear to be simple and straight and devoid of superstitions. On the teachings of Christianity and their efficacy, Raja Rammohun Roy said: "The simple code of religion, and morality is so admirably calculated to elevate men's ideas to high and liberal notions of one God, who has equally subjected all living creatures, without distinction of caste, rank or wealth, to change disappointment, pain and death, and has equally admitted all to be partakers of the bountiful mercies which he has lavished over nature, and is also so well fitted to regulate the conduct of the human race in discharge of their various duties to God, to themselves, and to society, that I cannot but hope the best effects from its promulgation in the present form."[14]

12 Iqbal Singh, *Rammohun Roy: Collected works*, p. 78.

13 Robert de. Baird (ed), *Religion in modern India*, p.173.

14 K. Nag and D. Burman, *The English works of Raja Rammohun Roy, Part I*, p. 4.

Since childhood Raja Rammohun Roy imbibed the best elements in Indian culture and religious tradition and did not deter from mastering some of the most difficult philosophers of the West. He took equal interest in the study of *Upaniṣads* as well as the writings of Aristotle, Herbert Spencer, Kant, Schopenhauer, J.S. Mill and the positivism of August Comte. Such a comparative study of the religious and intellectual heritage of the East and the West made him acutely aware of their contributions and drawbacks.[15]

The young Narendra Nath (his earlier name before he became a monk) associated himself with the movement of *Brahmo Samāj*. He liked the reformatory zeal of the *Brahmo* leaders. He read the works of Raja Rammohun Roy and admired the oratorical powers of Keshab Chandra Sen. He believed that *Brahmo Samāj* could remove the evils and superstitions from the Indian society. Hinduism needed a great cathartic agent to remove the wrong beliefs which became a part of it. The programme and action of the *Brahmo Samāj* enthused him. But later he felt that reform should come from within and not from without. He also realized that there was no use in picking faults with traditional beliefs and ideals of Indians. A country needs assimilation of ideas from every quarter of the world, but no nation could prosper if it just blindly imitates others. He considered that Hindu tradition and religion was rich enough in literature and religious ideas and had all the potential to emerge as a universal religion.[16]

Vivekananda gives an exposition of both the theoretical and practical aspects of *Vedānta*. For him, a theory which is incapable of being put into practice is worthless. The ideal of *Vedānta* lies in its practical aspects. The ideal and practical becomes one. Vivekananda initiates non-dualistic *Vedānta*

15 Ch. Srinivasa Rao, *Vedanta: Some modern trends*, pp. 88-89.

16 Ch. Srinivasa Rao, *Vedanta: Some modern trends*, p. 89.

which is of theoretical and practical value. He considered the *Vedānta* as a guiding principal not only for the people but also for the nations.[17]

> "The practical *Vedānta* of Vivekananda is an attempt to seek new applications of the essence and message of *Vedānta*. It holds, firstly, that all religions are expressions of the Ultimate Truth, and secondly, that the *Vedāntic* religion adopts the service of mankind which is essential."[18]

In order to propagate *Vedānta*, Vivekananda visualized the necessity of establishing a strong organization and training a batch of devoted souls to serve the masses. For him service of man was service of God. To propagate his ideas he founded Ramakrishna Math to train the novices into monastic order, and Ramakrishna Mission to propagate the ideals and to serve the people. Thus the Swami wanted to bring spiritual and social transformation.

The contemporary thinkers are sometimes called as neo-*Vedāntins*. They wanted to interpret *Vedānta* in the context of modern world. They wanted to build a system which should not disagree with the laws of science. They also felt that the individual should not stay away from the life and its activities after attaining the final realization. The realized soul should take active interest in improving the conditions of its fellow beings and practise the highest truths. The teachings of Vivekananda contain the synthesis of ancient Indian ideals and spiritual truths and the adoption of asceticism and monasticism, combined with humanitarianism and missionary work.[19] As Jawaharlal Nehru pointed out;

17 *Swami Vivekananda centenary volume*, P. 283.

18 McNicol, *The living religions of the Indian people*, pp. 110-118.

19 Sri Aurobindo, *Renaissance in India*, p. 46.

> "Vivekananda restated the wisdom of the ancient world in the light of the knowledge of the new world giving equal importance to the ancient and the modern."[20]

For Vivekananda, there is reconciliation between the ideal of renunciation and the duties of a house-holder. His emphasis on action and work has its source in the *Bhagavad Gītā* and is distinct from the Christian or Buddhist ideal of service motivated by love. Actions must be performed without any motive whatsoever. Vivekananda's interpretation of *Vedānta* opened new vistas, not only in the life of Indians, but also the entire humanity.[21]

Swami Vivekananda also gave importance to the concept of universal religion and considered that there was possibility of *Vedānta* becoming the universal religion. Like other Indian thinkers, he was also open-minded and cosmopolitan in his outlook. His ideas on Neo-*Vedānta* and social service were influenced by the Western culture. Though he was critical of certain Western ideas, he was at the same time appreciative of the contributions of Christianity and Western civilization.

Mahatma Gandhi

Perhaps no other contemporary Indian thinker has influenced the country and its course of direction as Mahatma Gandhi. He is considered as the Father of the Indian Nation. There were a large number of people who fought for the liberation of the country. But, Mahatma Gandhi gave a new direction to the freedom movement. Normally in any country, freedom struggle means fight between the ruler and the ruled. It is the common practice anywhere in the world from the dawn of history. But Mahatma Gandhi had brought in a new concept of *Satyāgraha* and he fought for India's freedom through non-violent means.

---

20 Jawaharlal Nehru, "Message of Swami Vivekananda to the modern world" in *Prabudda Bharata*, Volume, LXIX (1964).

21 Ch. Srinivas Rao, *Vedanta: Some modern trends*, p. 105

The Indian subcontinent was one of the biggest colonies of the British Empire. It was considered as the Crown Jewel of the British Empire. No colonial power wants to part with such a vast and prosperous country. Mahatma Gandhi believed in the potential goodness of man and also believed that people could know, one day or the other, what is proper and just. He continued his relentless struggle for the freedom of India through non-violence and made the British to concede freedom to India.

Mahatma Gandhi was a remarkable person. He was a freedom fighter as well as a religious and social reformer. The impact of Gandhi, like Karl Marx, is all-round. In simple terms, like Karl Marx, he had a distinct social, political, economic, religious and educational philosophy. Like other contemporary Indian thinkers, he was also English educated. He went to England and studied law. He was exposed to all modern social and political ideologies. The new trends in religion also appealed him. He studied Christianity thoroughly when he was in England, with all humility and receptivity. At one stage his British friends wanted him to convert to Christianity. But Mahatma Gandhi considered that one's respect and love for a religion need not make one to convert into it. His love for Hinduism was great. But at the same time, he had also great respect for Christianity. He also studied other religions like Islam and Zoroastrianism. He used to have regular correspondence with Leo Tolstoy, the famous Russian writer and eminent Christian thinker. Thus Gandhi was exposed to all religions and he imbibed the spirit of those religions and cultures.

Mahatma Gandhi believed that theory and practice should go together and in whatever principles and theories he believed, he wanted to put them in to practice. He considered that *Satyāgraha*, non-violence and love should be the basis for all human interactions. The study of Mahatma Gandhi's ideas and their impact on India as well as the world and their relevance are note-worthy. Radhakrishnan writes:

> "In my travels to different parts of World I have noted that Gandhi's reputation is more universal than that of the greatest statesmen and leaders of nation, and his personality is more beloved and esteemed than any or all of them. His name is familiar to such a degree that there is scarcely present a factory worker who does not consider him to be friend of humankind."[22]

Unlike other thinkers, Mahatma Gandhi faced gigantic problems. During his lifetime the world was full of upheavals. There were two World Wars and also he saw the emergence of new ideologies like Nazism, Fascism and Marxism. The world was pulled apart by these powerful ideologies.

It was the time when great strides were made in science and technology. The atom was split and a lethal and powerful device called atom bomb was made to subdue Japan, the Americans dropped two atom bombs—one on Hiroshima and another on Nagasaki—and the Japanese surrendered and the Second World War came to an end. The atom bomb was such a destructive weapon that more than one lakh people died on that day of bombing and almost the same number died later due to atomic radiation. This event was another great challenge to Mahatma Gandhi who believed in *ahiṃsā* (non-violence). Thus we find pacifism on one side and violence and horror on the other. This is a new challenge to the doctrines of Mahatma Gandhi.

Throughout the world, there is a dialogue regarding the doctrines of Mahatma Gandhi, and the doctrines of political power and violence. Lot of discussions are going on regarding the relevance of the philosophy of Mahatma Gandhi.

Radhakrishnan

Radhakrishnan was an eminent philosopher, statesman and academician. He was one of the greatest thinkers of 20th century. Beginning his career as a teacher, he rose to highest

22 S. Radhakrishnan (ed), *Mahatma Gandhi: Essays and reflections.* pp. 28-29.

positions—the Vice President and President of India. He is considered as one of the great scholar-statesmen of India. He was prolific writer and considered as the bridge between the East and the West. When there was diffidence among India and among the people about the greatness of their culture, Radhakrishnan made them to know about their great heritage. No nation can become prosperous unless it is proud of its own culture and heritage. All great nations and eminent powers became so because of their people's patriotism and their pride for their past. Radhakrishnan wanted Indian people to be proud of their heritage. But at the same time, he said that we should not neglect to imbibe and accept the noble values of other cultures.

Radhakrishnan himself was a happy blend of the East and the West. He had his education in the best Christian schools and colleges and he was inspired by the Christian values inculcated in these citadels of learning. He himself worked in Oxford University and interacted with the great minds of the West. Thus we find Radhakrishnan taking all that was great and good from the East and West. He wanted to see India becoming a prosperous and peaceful nation standing as equal to other nations of the world. Like Bertrand Russell, he took keen interest in all social, political and economic issues of the time and also had great concern for the future of human civilization. Thus he was a nationalist and an internationalist. In Radhakrishnan, India had produced academic philosopher whose stature is not less than that of any other contemporary philosopher of Europe or America. J.H. Muirhead said Bergson and Radhakrishnan occupy similar positions as leaders of thought in Europe and India.[23]

Radhakrishnan's originality consisted in depth with which he grasped the significance of what he said and made it dominate over the details. E.S. Brightman hailed

23 Hibbert, *Journal*, October. 1912.

Radhakrishnan as "one of the greatest philosophers of mysticism in modern times."[24] Radhakrishnan held that philosophy was an attempt to co-ordinate and interpret all experience and understand the world as a whole, to say that it should take into account and explain integral experience as well as the discoveries of science which may not contradict each other.

Radhakrishnan says that the development and progress of any country is not simply based on economic growth. A country should always have certain goals to achieve and on the basis of those goals only its reconstruction programme should be taken up. Radhakrishnan wanted that India should be receptive to new ideas from the West and should adopt those to suit Indian conditions. He was a fine product of the best values of the East and the West. Due to the impact of Indian Renaissance and his family background, he was equally proud of his Indian heritage.

Contemporary Indian thinkers were unique and distinct in their own way. Out of these only Radhakrishnan had thorough academic background. He was a teacher, scholar and academician. But at the same time, like other thinkers, he was influenced by the Indian Renaissance. He wanted to reform Indian society and wanted that it should have its proper place in the comity of nations. The Catholicity of Indian culture is such that it is liberal and appreciative of other cultures. It never considered that truth is the exclusive position of Hinduism. Truth is one but it is expressed in different ways by different cultures. The famous adage says that, *Ekam Sat Viprā Bahudā Vadanti* (Truth is one but the wisemen express it in different ways). Thus, Radhakrishnan believes that one should be liberal in his attitude towards religion. The purpose of religion is the liberation of individuals (souls) and it is possible through all religions.

---

24 P. A. Schilpp (ed), *The philosophy of Radhakrishnan*, p. 414.

In the second chapter the *Brahmo Samāj* movement and its impact on Indian society are discussed. Like other Indian thinkers, he considered about the possibility of *Vedānta* becoming a universal religion. He discussed about the reason and revelation on which generally every philosopher wants to express his ideas. Like a true *Vedāntin* who gives importance to the concept of *Nirguṇa Brahman,* he opposes idol worship. He also rejects the doctrine of incarnation.

The thrid chapter deals with the religious views of Swami Vivekananda who had given a new direction to *Vedānta* and infused the spirit of nationalism and patriotism in the people. He mixed religion and nationalism. He considered that the reconstruction and reformation of India was possible only through the understanding of the true spirit of *Vedānta.* He made the Indians proud of their heritage and culture, and wanted to make India come out of its deep slumber. This chapter contains his views on religion, the divine nature of man and his concept of universal religion. Like Rammohun Roy, he also believed that through *Vedānta* and its practice many of the evils of India could be removed.

Swami Vivekananda was not only a great spiritualist but also an eminent scholar, well versed in the philosophies of both the West and the East. He also considered that *Vedānta* had the possibility of becoming a universal religion. Though he was critical of the methods adopted by some missionaries for conversion, he was highly appreciative of what Christianity had done to the world. The spirit of service to the mankind is the product of Christian religious and philosophical values. Sri Ramakrishna Mission and its ideals of social service owe much to the Christian spirit of service. An assessment is also made in the end about Swami Vivekananda's contribution to the Indian Renaissance.

The fourth chapter deals with the ideas of Mahatma Gandhi on religion. Gandhi was a religious man. From his early childhood we find the deep impact of religion on him. Though he went to England for his legal studies, he maintained his religious fervor. In England, he came into contact with many eminent Christian scholars and he studied seriously the tenets of Christianity and also other religions. In Mahatma Gandhi we find a leader who did not give up religion even in secular and political pursuits. When we study about freedom fighters and eminent statesmen, we find their religious ideas and convictions relegated to the background. But in Mahatma Gandhi we find religion in the centre around which all other endeavors veer around.

The innovative ideas of Mahatma Gandhi on basic issues of religion like God, faith, worship, ethics, liberation and society are dealt in detail in this chapter. Mahatma Gandhi considered that religious convictions should make us good citizens, and also good human beings. His comparative study of different religions made him convinced that the aim of every religion was to make us foster good conduct and accept that there is common goal of liberation. Gandhi wanted to bring freedom to India through *Satyāgraha* and non-violence. He wanted to give a spiritual thrust to his political movement.

India is a multi-religious country. All the world religions like Buddhism, Islam and Christianity have their followers in millions. The British not only ruled India but also influenced the Indian society through its educational system, culture and religion. Mahatma Gandhi studied the tenets of Christianity very deeply while he was in England and it has shaped his religious attitude. He considered that the Sermon on the Mount is a great message and mankind should be shaped as per the Sermon. Though he loved Hinduism in which he was born, he had great veneration for other religions and mainly Christianity. All eminent thinkers have expressed their views on religious pluralism and universal religion. Mahatma Gandhi's views on this aspect of religion are also thought-provoking. Thus this chapter gives a comprehensive analysis of Mahatma Gandhi's religious ideas.

The fifth chapter deals with the religious thought of Dr. Sarvepalli Radhakrishnan. Unlike the other thinkers about whom we have discussed, Radhakrishnan was basically an academician and a scholar. His reflections on world religions are profound. He studied Hinduism and Indian philosophy deeply and tried to interpret its tenets on the basis of modern science. Like other thinkers about whom we have discussed, Radhakrishnan also felt that religion had a very vital role to play everywhere. Due to the developments of science and technology, the social systems are facing new problems. Man is alienated and he is in search of identity. Radhakrishnan feels that man can find solace only through religion, whether it is Hinduism, Christianity, Buddhism or Islam.

The religious thought of Radhakrishnan and his views on Christianity have been analyzed. The basic concepts of religions are also briefly analyzed in this chapter. Discussion on challenges to religion through secularism and Marxism also find place in the chapter. Radhakrishnan has elaborately dealt with the concepts like intuition and intellect, religious experience and the relation between religion and ethics, religion and society, religion and science, religious tolerance, etc.

The sixth chapter which is a summary and conclusion of the study briefly summarizes all the chapters on the contemporary Indian thinkers. As a whole they wanted to rejuvenate and reform Indian society. They felt that such resurgence was possible only through revival of true religious spirit and inculcation of its values in Indian society.

2

Raja Rammohun Roy

Raja Rammohun Roy was born on 22 May 1772, at Radhanagar, a village in the Hoogly District in West Bengal. His parents were Ramakanta Roy and Tarinidevi. At the age of 17, he witnessed the French Revolution. From the beginning he studied the Indian and the European classics and for this purpose, he learned many languages. To read the *Bible* in original he learned Hebrew language. After getting enough knowledge in almost all fields, he wanted to start both religious and social reformations in India. He studied Arab scientists, and philosophers like Plato, Aristotle and Plotinus. He later shifted to Benaras for Sanskrit studies. His life comes into clearer focus by the time he is thirty.[25] Within few years he mastered all the Hindu scriptures, especially the *Upaniṣads*. In 1802, he went to Mursirabad, a well known centre for Islamic culture, and further continued his Arabic studies. He wrote his first book *Tuhfat-ul-Muwahhideen* (gifts for monotheists).

Raja Rammohun Roy mainly focused towards reforms within the Hinduism. In 1828, he established the *Brahmo Samāj*. The real mission was realization of God in every human being. He made great campaign against evil practices of Hinduism, particularly *Satī*. The main target of Raja Rammohun Roy was idol worship. He was the greatest personality of Indian Renaissance. On the night of 27 September 1833, he breathed his last at 2.25.a.m.[26] He was the leader of new

25 Arvind Sharma, *Modern Hindu thought*, p. 5.

26 Mrs. Suman Prem Kumar, *Raja Rammohun Roy*, p. 46.

movement in Indian thought, tried to distinguish what was valuable in Indian tradition. He boldly advocated against traditionalism. He pleaded for supply of scientific books, instruments and setting up of laboratories. President Dr. S. Radhakrishnan in his speech said, Raja Rammohun Roy stood for equality against caste, for science against superstitions, for democracy against dictatorship, for religion of truth and not a religion of superstition.

As Rabindranath Tagore said, the man who ushered in the modern epoch in India was Raja Rammohun Roy, who may also be considered as the father of modern Indian philosophy. The social legislation which from time to time sought to modernize Hindu society and which ultimately culminated in a uniform law for all Hindus was the outcome of the movement started by Raja Rammohun Roy.

In the context of modern Hinduism, Raja Rammohun Roy was among the first figures to make the sacred texts freely available to people both in the original and with translations, and who, taking his stand on them, questioned idol worship, worked for the abolition of *Satī* and threw his weight in favour of the introduction of Western science. He learned English in later life and was soon defending his version of Hinduism against the version given by Christian missionaries. These public religious activities culminated in the founding of a place of worship in 1828, called the *Brahmo Samāj*, where worship proceeded as follows:

Two Telugu *Brāhmins* used to recite the *Vedas* in a side-room, screened from the view of the congregation, where non-*Brāhmins* would not be admitted: Utsavananda would read texts of the *Upaniṣads*, which were afterwards explained in Bengali by Pundit Ram Chandra Vidyavagish, who would then preach or read the sermons, some of which were written by Raja Rammohun Roy.

Brahmo Samāj

Raja Rammohun Roy was the leading figure in the awakening of modern India. He has rightly been described as the father of Indian Renaissance. Deeply devoted to the work of religious and social reform, he laid the foundation of *Brahmo Samāj* on August 20, 1828[27] as a protest against certain orthodox beliefs, unnecessary rituals and superstitions of Hinduism such as idol worship, polygamy, child marriage, enforced widowhood and social ostracism of those who crossed the black water. The reaction of Indian resurgence was moral and social rather than political. He brought about the abolition of *Satī*—the cruel practice of burning the Hindu widow on the funeral pyre of her dead husband. He justified his views by the light of reason and humanitarian principles. He accepted the *Upaniṣads* as his authority and declared the fact that man can realize the spiritual goal of his life by means of meditation of the divine and not by sacrificial rituals. His aim was to promote monotheistic worship and adoration of the one Eternal Immutable God with the abolition of consciousness and recognition of equality of women. The *Brahmo Samāj* is firmly rooted in the *Vedas*, the *Upanishads* and the *Brahma Sūtra*. But at the same time, it is ready to break the tradition.

As a Universalist, he stands for the solidarity of religions. He preached a rational approach to religions by reading the scriptures of other religions with a view to discover the fundamental unity of all religions. He showed how the essential values of the great Indian heritage were to be preserved and how the non-essentials were to be discarded. His conclusion is that there are successive stages of growth and degeneration of each religion and consequently falsehood is common to all religions without distinction.

He had adopted the process of elimination of the crude stages of each religion, which was essential for the survival of religions and for the social progress. According to him, the

27 Dev Raj Bali, *Modern Indian thought*, p. 9.

Universal Religion can be formed by filtering the common truths of Hinduism, Islam, Christianity and other faiths. The creed he had formed is called Neo-Theo-Philanthropy, a New Love God and Man.

Raja Rammohun Roy found many social evils and superstitions in Hinduism. He wanted to purify it by the help of modern knowledge and science. He believed that the outmoded customs and religious dogmatism and fanaticism were represented by reactionary social forces. They were introduced by the one section of the society for their own sake to exploit the masses. There was no caste distinction at the time of the *Vedas*. By understanding the *Vedas* properly misconceptions can be cleared. Along with his own religion, Raja Rammohun Roy had accepted both Islam and Christianity with some limitations. Both had exerted a profound influence on his mind. But he never followed them blindly. He rejected both as far as irrational and unscientific elements were concerned in them as in the case of Hinduism. He wholeheartedly prepared to accept the moral principles of the *New Testament* and completely rejected the *Old Testament*. He also opposed the Christian missionaries, their attitude and their attempt at proselytisation.

He was bold enough to complain that the British rulers were intentionally violating their pledge of religious neutrality by encouraging Christian missionaries to write books ridiculing the Hindu and Muslim faiths. At the same time, he vehemently opposed many customs and beliefs of the Hindu society. He did not accept the prevalent dogmas of the Hindus regarding their numerous gods and rituals. He did not accept their concept of rebirth and *avatāras*, their practice of idol worship, animal sacrifice and the most inhuman and the barbarous practice of *Satī*. He believed that Hinduism was rooted in a broad humanist outlook. Hinduism is swept away by the cobwebs of superstitions which have accumulated through the ages. He wanted Hinduism to regenerate as a truly national religion suited to the new conditions of social life. Without accepting polytheism and polytheistic ritualism, he supported monism (a philosophical theory that all beings may ultimately be referred to one category) and propagated it in his teachings.

He believed that there is only one Eternal Being. He used *Vedāntic* Monism as a weapon in his struggle against orthodoxy and to raise the people to a higher and noble life. He also tried to form a universal religion based on faith in the single God and the cognition of human values. He called upon the people to give a polytheistic ritualism and requested them to worship and keep faith in only one pure Formless God. He tried to make the people to recognize the Divine Spark in every human being. He believed that Monism was nothing but the symbol of India's unity in diversity.

The propagation of religious teachings of Raja Rammohun Roy followed the rich and everlasting heritage of the humanistic outlook of Kabir, Chaitanya, Ravidas and other saints of the Bhakti Movement, which was itself based on *Upaniṣadic* Monism propounded by great thinkers of India like Ramanuja and Ramananda. In one sense, the reformation initiated by Raja Rammohun Roy is nothing but a continuation of the *bhakti* Movement. He took the help of the Monotheistic outlook of both Islam and Christianity to strengthen his belief in Monism. In this regard, he wanted to assimilate the new values created by Western science and tried to synthesize them with the traditional values of India so as to meet the challenges of the new age. He believed that no progress is possible without proper change.

Raja Rammohun Roy was an absolutely independent thinker and committed theist, besides a rationalist and devoted moralist. He wholeheartedly accepted the ethical principles of Christianity and rejected the divinity of Jesus Christ just as he rejected the concept of incarnations in Hindu philosophy. He also rejected the most important concept of Trinity in

Christianity, which is the heart and soul of it. Because of these progressive noble ideas, he faced a lot of controversies both from Hindus and Christians. But he never compromised with them. He boldly attacked them and never accepted their views as far as religious ideas are concerned.

He founded the Bengali journal *Sambad Kaumudi* (moon light) in 1821 and the Persian paper *Ulakbar* in 1882 to carry out the message of national awakening. In spite of a number of restrictions by the British Government on them, finally he succeeded in his campaign. He spread the message of national renaissance to all parts of the country. He campaigned vigorously against caste system, idol worship, animal sacrifice, etc. He wanted to spread the spirit of humanism and universal brotherhood.

The medieval custom known as *Satī* which, forced widows to commit suicide by jumping into the funeral pyres of their husbands, was still prevalent in some parts of the country, especially in Bengal, Rajasthan and Uttar Pradesh. Raja Rammohun Roy himself had the shocking experience of helplessly watching the sacrifice of his own sister-in-law on the funeral pyre of his own brother. After a long struggle, at last in 1829, the British Government under the supervision of Lord William Bentinck made *Satī* illegal. According to Raja Rammohun Roy, there is no *Vedic* sanction for it. Besides the eradication of *Satī*, Roy paid special attention to remove the inequalities between men and women. He fought for equal property rights for women. He campaigned vigorously in favour of widow remarriages and against child marriages and fought for their education and their introduction in all walks of life. He gave his powerful support to the introduction of modern education. Along with his friends, he started a number of educational institutions for the promotion of modern education which was a synthesis of Eastern and Western values.

Vedānta

Raja Rammohun Roy was the first Indian to take scholarly interest in *Vedānta* in early nineteenth century. He published translations of the *Upaniṣads* and commentary on the *Vedānta Sūtras* in Bengali and English languages. He had the privilege of introducing and popularizing the *Vedāntic* scriptures amongst his countrymen, and the people of other nationalities. His interest in the *Vedic* scripture is not to be regarded as a purely scholarly venture, but to be taken as the testimony of a man who had faith in *Vedānta*. He showed great interest in Sankaracharya, whose commentary on the *Upaniṣads* was adopted by him as the text for the translation of different *Upaniṣads*.

To know Raja Rammohun Roy's *Vedānta*, one has to take into account the ideas which he admired in Hinduism and other religions. As there is no unanimity in the interpretation of the *Vedāntic* philosophers, and such differing views cannot be fully resolved even by going back to the *Vedic* scripture, *Upaniṣads* and the *Vedānta Sūtras*. In spite of the fact that the basic text followed by the *Vedāntins* remains identical, the development and conclusions of the theme of the *Vedānta* take different forms. Like all scriptures, the basic works of *Vedānta* are the products of thought and outpourings of seers and mystics, who did not cast their ideas in clear language. So the *Upaniṣads* gave scope for diverse interpretations, so are the *Sūtras*.

Raja Rammohun Roy took upon himself the responsibility to write a commentary on the *Vedānta Sūtras*, with the intention of showing the glorious side of Indian thought and religion. He believed that, once his countrymen become acquainted with the ancient literature, they would give up all the superstitions and evil practices, as none of them is supported by the ancient scripture. It is through the medium of *Vedānta* that Raja Rammohun Roy wanted to retrieve his countrymen from the mire of retrogressive beliefs which were put into circulation by persons who were concerned more with their selfish gains than the good of the people.

The Indian medievalism is first reflected in the belief of abstract universalism of the *Vedāntic* school, which does not accept any characteristics or qualities in the Divinity. This universalism aims to dissociate senses, mind, emotions and will of men from the external worlds and society.

He wanted to eradicate ceremonialism and idol worship with the help of *Vedānta*. But his *Vedānta* was not confined to the belief in abstract universalism. For him, the Absolute or Brahman is to be known through *tatasthalakṣaṇa*, i.e. Brahman in relation to the universe. *Brahman* has both transcendental and immanent aspects. Raja Rammohun Roy attempts to synthesize, on the ground of reason and rationality, the elements contained in both Sankara and Ramanuja.[28]

Vedāntic Universalism

Raja Rammohun Roy recapitulates the salient feature of *Vedānta*. *Vedānta* represents to him the totality of the meaning contained in the Vedic scripture, which was reduced into a terse form in the *Vedānta Sūtras*. His *Vedāntic* thought is not an isolated phenomenon unconnected with the thinkers of *Vedānta* preceding or following him.[29]

Raja Rammohun Roy attempted to inculcate the ideas of *Vedānta* in the place of those beliefs which were retrogressive and opposed to moral canons. He opposed those dogmas which preached escapism from life's demands. His thought influenced India, similar to that of Bacon on Europe. He brings out the elements of a new humanism and pleads for the basing of all human relations and different institutions on the principles of justice and benevolence. He wanted his country men to

28 Ch. Srinivasa Rao, *Vedanta: Some modern trends*, p. 38.

29 *Ibid.*, p. 54.

understand the scripture and follow the message of *Vedānta*. For him, reason is the potent guide to help one reach the position of *Vedānta*. Where reason prevails, superstitions cannot reign; similarly, to know the spirit of *Vedānta* is to identify oneself with all that which stands for human good and progress. *Vedānta* was the bulwark which prepared Raja Rammohun Roy to undertake a mighty reformation in society, religion and philosophy. It can be said that his progressive outlook was sustained by his deep insight into the ancient scripture and *Vedānta* literature.

Brahman, the Supreme Being

Raja Rammohun Roy gave great importance to the work of Vyāsa and thought that, had the Hindus understood it, they would not have been misled by harmful notions.[30] Vyāsa aimed at providing true knowledge about the nature of the Supreme. The One Supreme is the sole object of study in the *Vedas*. That the One is beyond the reach of senses and the comprehension of men is acknowledged by the *Upaniṣads*. Following the *Upaniṣadic* view that the Supreme One cannot be properly described by any scripture or text, Vyāsa advocates that the Supreme is indefinable, indescribable.

Brahman has no equal. The comprehension of *Brahman* is by acquainting oneself deeply with the products created by Him.[31] Raja Rammohun Roy finds in the second text, first chapter of the *Vedānta Sūtras*, that the Supreme Being is the source of all multiform ties. The Supreme One is the great regulating force of all that happens and will happen in the universe. The world has its emergence from the Supreme Being. Roy does not agree with those who think that an indescribable Supreme should not be regarded as the cause of everything in the universe. The thesis that the Indefinable Supreme is the Creator, Sustainer and Destroyer of the universe is supported by the *Vedānta Sūtras*.[32]

30 Ch. Srinivasa Rao, *Vedanta: Some modern trends*, p. 38.

31 Ramakrishna Rao, V. *Rammohun and larger unites of life*, F.M.I. Pt.II p. 361.

32 Ch. Srinivasa Rao, *Vedanta: Some modern trends*, p. 39.

Raja Rammohun Roy develops his monotheism on the basis of the *Upaniṣadic* assumption that the Supreme is one and besides Him, there can be no other cause of the universe.[33] As the controlling force, the Supreme only is responsible for the appearance of everything. To know this truth about the Supreme is to acquire great perfection and eternal bliss. Those who have no idea of the nature of the Supreme cannot hope to attain spiritual perfection. Raja Rammohun Roy mentions that, according to *Bṛhadāraṇyaka Upaniṣad*, both the final truth and the real knowledge rest with the Supreme Being.

That the Supreme is the knower of everything, the embodiment of truth, formless, indescribable and eternal, is advocated by *Chāndogya Upaniṣad*. The acceptance of the Supreme Being as omniscient and formless implies that anything which is describable is not to be regarded as the cause of the universe. The monotheism of Raja Rammohun Roy accepts the indescribable Supreme as separate yet connected with material things. The Supreme is different yet connected with everything in creation, says Raja Rammohun Roy. Commenting on *Vedānta Sūtras* III. 2. 16, Raja Rammohun Roy points out that *Brahman* is not describable, yet He is one with the smallest and the greatest. *Brahman* is both transcendent and immanent. The *Vedānta Sutras* II.1.30 states that, there are present the attributes of highest excellence in God and hence the indescribable Brahman is describable through reason. Raja Rammohun Roy accepts the conception of *Śvetāsvetara Upaniṣad* VI. 8 that God is the highest and the supreme. The Supreme Being is the Originator and Governor of the universe and is present in the universe.

***Brahman* and the World**

Raja Rammohun Roy adopts the view that God is both efficient and material cause of the universe, following *Vedānta Sūtras* I.4.23: Like a potter who shapes pots, God creates everything.

33 Ch. Srinivasa Rao, *Vedanta: Some modern trends*, p. 42.

Like clay which is common to all pots, God is material cause of all objects. He quotes the famous simile of the spider and web from *Muṇḍaka Upaniṣad*,[34] to show that God is the material and efficient cause of everything in the universe. The indefinable formless Supreme is the ultimate material and efficient cause and that which resembles Him is clearly not the primary cause, says Roy.

Individual Soul

Raja Rammohun Roy maintains that the individual soul is having its origin in the Supreme Spirit. This makes the soul share a number of such qualities which can only be attributed to the Supreme. Neither the world nor the human soul is illusory for Roy. The human soul is a necessary adjunct and it is the focus of God manifestation. To know God, the soul needs not disappear into nothingness, but needs gradual enfoldment and complete surrender to Him. God is the inner soul of every being and by worshipping God, man would be the recipient of Divine grace. When the potentialities of human soul grow in dimension the way is open for God-realization. The omniscience and omnipresence of God should not be made the basis for the assumption that the soul is created from nothing.[35]

The soul is sentient and capable of realizing its likeness with the Supreme. It is the mover of the body and senses but is itself dependent on the All-pervading Spirit. The individual soul is not to be taken as the same as the Supreme Spirit which is present everywhere.

Hence it follows that the individual soul is only a humble subject before the Lord of the universe. The individual gains all perfections and is the recipient of infinite bliss, when it realizes

---

34 *Muṇḍaka Upaniṣad*, I.I.7.

35 *Brahmanical magazine*, E.W.Pt.II, p. 147.

its unity and likeness with the Supreme. If the world emanates from God, the whole creation is to be taken as dependent on and supported by Him.[36]

The external world and the soul being parts of creation are co-equals in creation. The soul in association with the body acts as the controller of the body. The sense organs and the apparatus of the body need the guidance of the soul which is the centre of sentience. The soul in connection with the body is placed amidst different adjuncts, but once freed from its association with the body, it will revert to the Original Sources. Raja Rammohun Roy thinks that the being of man is not devoid of divine elements, it can be said that the sentient soul coming out of Supreme Spirit shares the essence of the Supreme. Nothing occurs or exists in the universe without the will of the Supreme.

Significance of Moral Ideals

The human desire to know the Supreme is not free from moral ideas. The relation between man and the Supreme can be illustrated on the basis of moral ideals:

> "The *Vedānta Sūtras* III.4.27, plead for the catharsis of the instinctual desires and proclivities, so that body and mind of man may attain purity to realize the likeness with the Supreme."[37]

Man has to nurture morality with great care, in order to accomplish the ultimate goal of realizing the Supreme. To tread the moral path is more difficult than the following of the natural propensities. Man is to be the master of his energies, inner propensities and desires and follows only the spirit of the scripture, says Raja Rammohun Roy. Man should surrender

36 Chowdari, Dhirendranath –*Vedantavais, Dharmer Tattwa, O; Sadan*, p. 239.

37 Deussen, Paul, *The philosophy of the Upanishads*, p. 61.

himself to the Supreme, seeking life from Him. To have firm knowledge of the Supreme is to have undiluted bliss, wisdom and joy.

Religion

Religion occupies a prominent place in Raja Rammohun Roy's thought. The concept of religion which he developed has within it some of the most significant generalizations arrived at by the *Vedic* thinkers as well as the founders of Semitic religions.[38] Religion is the domain wherein the human spirit comes into its own and becomes reflective of that which is the source of everything. It also makes man aware of the All-pervading Spirit which originates and sustains every product in the universe. Raja Rammohun Roy's definition of religion is an integral synthesis of the dominant standpoints of world's major religions. Raja Rammohun Roy does not toy with the idea of religion in a nonchalant way, as for him the aim of religion is comprehensive enough to initiate man into the secrets of the mystery surrounding him.

It is in the field of religion that man comes to assert himself as the being who has the potentiality to unravel the depths of the Unknown.[39] Raja Rammohun Roy's life itself is an annotation of the term religion. His life not only exemplifies the theme of religion but also is a saga of a man who tried to show the essence of religion. Roy thinks that religion is not a code of morality, nor is it concerned with the persistent theological problems; for religion has a more practical bearing on the life and existence of man and has to play a vital role in man's adjustment to his environment.

According to Raja Rammohun Roy, religion is a prime force which has given decisive shape to the history of man. Under the impact of religion, man shaped and developed the various laws

38 Muller Max. F., *Biographical eassys*, p. 3.

39 Chowdhuri, Dhirendranath, *Vedanta Vagis, Dharmer Tattwa O!* Sadan, p. 232.

which were meant to govern his activities. Even the earliest man arrived at the idea of a great power which determines the shape and course of everything in the cosmos. Beneath the most crude expressions of the earliest man, there is present the idea of an Omniscient Being or Beings as responsible for the production of the great cosmic drama whose central figure is none other than man. As Raja Rammohun Roy thinks that the being of man is resplendent with Divine elements, it is but natural that he should have always attempted to know the nature of the Supreme Being. According to Raja Rammohun Roy:

> "Man can hardly escape from being religious, once he starts thinking on the substratum of the universe; and the nature of his being. He says that the major scriptures of the world have unanimously supported certain themes and in recapitulating and meditating those themes, one can grasp the kernel of religion."[40]

The approach of Raja Rammohun Roy towards religion makes it clear that he did not accept any set of dogmatic beliefs as correct only because they were in vogue since times immemorial. His definition of religion is a protest against antiquated ideas, but not certainly a rejection of everything which is old and rooted in the earliest beginning of human civilization and thought.[41] His emphasis on the relevance of religion in the life of man would ultimately remove the impediments in the growth of the society and polity on the lines of justice and equity.

To understand Raja Rammohun Roy's concept of religion, it is not enough to know the genesis and development of Hinduism. It would also be incorrect to say that only Islam or Christianity can help one fully appreciate Roy's concept of religion. It is at the confluence of the best traditions of Christianity, Islam, Hinduism and other religions that Roy stands.[42]

---

40 Ch. Srinivasa Rao, *Vedanta: Some modern trends*, p. 58.

41 Muller Max. F., *India: What can it teach us*? p. 249.

42 *Modern India*. F.M.I.Pt.II, p. 71.

The religion of Raja Rammohun Roy can hardly be given a label or a name. Had he been fully satisfied with the religions which he so earnestly studied, he would have espoused the cause of one or the other, instead of founding the *Brahmo Samāj*. It does not mean that for him the major religions are devoid of genuine content. It is essential to note that by starting *Brahmo Samāj*, he was setting a corrective principle which can set right the perspectives of the followers of different religions, so that in the light of the ideology of the *Brahmo Samāj*, they could undertake a fresh re-appraisal of the religious ideas believed by them fervently.

Hence the *Brahmo Samāj* was not intended to replace any existing religion but only aimed to project a set of religious ideas which were universal and catholic in their tone and content. According to Raja Rammohun Roy, true religion means:

> "The perpetuation of the attributes of One Supreme Being, fraternity and brotherhood of men, the sublimity of the moral action and the supremacy of human conscience and reason. It is on the basis of these ideas that the movement of *Brahmo Samāj* was born and this movement can be taken as the focal point of Roy's concept of religion."[43]

Social Reforms

Raja Rammohun Roy makes it clear that true religion cannot harbor within it superstitious beliefs. It is from the plane of religion that he initiates a number of social reforms.[44] He knew that beneath the actions and practices of men are present the complex of beliefs and ideas. Legislation can, no doubt, counteract any practice which is outrageous to human dignity and freedom, but legislation alone cannot change the beliefs

---

43 Sen, Keshab Chunder, F.M.I.Pt.II, p. 182.

44 Sastri, Sivanath, *The history of Brahmo Samaj*, Vol.I. pp. 2, 3.

in the minds of men. It can be done only by systematically demonstrating that many beliefs held by people are against the spirit of the sacred scriptures.[45]

Due to the impact of Raja Rammohun Roy's writing and translations of the religious scriptures in the language of the people, a silent revolution took place in Indian society and instead of professing faith in obsolete and wrong beliefs, people became aware of ideas which were religious and progressive. Raja Rammohun Roy has defended himself against the charges of being an infidel. He says that he has always upheld the position of *Vedānta* theology, hence cannot be accused of committing any heresy. He makes it clear that in the field of religion he has never tried to make any innovations and that it has been his ardent wish to represent the pure religion of the *Vedas*.

Reason and Revelation

In the *Vedas, Purāṇas, Tantras* and Hindu mythology, Raja Rammohun Roy finds enough rational elements delineating a system of theism which is self-consistent and non-contradictory.[46] The ideas which are a part of Hindu religion and are rooted in the ancient scriptures are rational as well as universal. Such aspects of Hindu religion attract the attention of Raja Rammohun Roy. The assertions that men are equal, that the Divine can be realized by everyman, that religious and moral acts invoke the benediction of God, made Hinduism a tolerant religion. Hinduism as visualized by Raja Rammohun Roy is based on ancient texts.

The scriptures insist on the need to worship the Divine in a pure way, since all idolatry is due to lack of correct understanding of the scripture. It is difficult to justify idolatry by arguing that every idol represents an attribute of the

45 Panikkar, K.M. *Hinduism and the modern world,* p. 13.

46 *The Brahmanical magazine, E.W. Pt.* II. p. 153

Supreme Being. Those who worship idols firmly believe that every idol is representing a deity and possessing Divine power. Each particular God is ascribed with a set of characteristics and treated as independent and separate from other divinities. Mythology grows around every God:

> "The worshipers of Śiva and Viṣṇu would seldom agree that the images of gods are only mediums to elevate the mind to conceive the nature of the Supreme, and instead every idol would be regarded by its followers as superior to the rest."[47]

The *Śāstras* admit that for persons who are not capable of meditating on the Indivisible Supreme Being, some form or object is necessary for adoration and worship. It has to be accepted that human mind does not lack the capacity to conceive the nature of the Supreme Being in lieu of idols.

Universal Religion

Raja Rammohun Roy's theism, based on the uncompromising doctrine of the One God, is indicative of universal religion. His theism is an assertion and elaboration of identical views in different religions concerning the Supreme God.[48] Since his theism does not suffer from the overtones of Hinduism, Christianity or Islam, it should not be regarded as an exemplification of any particular religion, but the concepts found in the basic scriptures.

Raja Rammohun Roy arrives at the concept of universal religion, after gaining full acquaintance with the theories and dogmas of religions like Christianity, Hinduism and Islam. He agrees with the idea that by following one's own religion, one can arrive at the understanding that the essence of all religions lies in the acceptance of One Divinity. Raja Rammohun Roy

---

47 Preface *Isopanishad*, E.W.Pt.II. p. 45.

48 Seal Brajendranath, *Rammohun Roy, the universal man*, p. 18.

does not maintain that one needs to forego his own religion and tradition and adopt a new creed containing within it the elements which go into the making of the universal religion.[49]

Raja Rammohun Roy's main interest is to make human beings more human. He reintroduces the religious person to his own religion by bringing out the essential content and principles of the religion followed. The best in every religion is taken by Raja Rammohun Roy and by mutual comparison the universality of the religious theme is established. Men belonging to different nationalities, races, and creeds, by virtue of their professing faith in One Invisible Supreme, may be regarded as belonging to a Universal Church. The *Brahmo Samāj* of Raja Rammohun Roy indicates the Universal Church, which is the common place of worship for the believers in One God, even though they may be professing different religions.

Raja Rammohun Roy finds the moral principles contained in the *New Testament* to be of great significance. He thinks that by practising such moral maxims alone the man is spiritually regenerated. Raja Rammohun Roy accepts:

> "The possibility of the transformation of man, under the impact of moral precepts, emphasizes on the necessity of living the very essence of the moral precepts."[50]

By taking moral precepts as essential constituents of religion, he makes religion more humanitarian and deeply concerned with the equality, dignity and sanctity of the human personality. His religion contains the two strands of the humanism and spirituality, wherein man emerges as a spiritual being whose source and origin lies in the Invisible Resplendent God.

Raja Rammohun Roy maintains that the revival of the pure religious spirit and dependence on inductive reason would

---

49 Seal Brajendranath, *Rammohun Roy, the universal man*, p. 103.

50 Precepts of Jesus ...... E.W.Pt. V.P.4.

make people aware of the futility of accepting the supernatural explanations. By believing in supernatural occurrences of miracles, the capacity to think clearly is destroyed. The reign of supernaturalism has destroyed the right perspective of man in religious matters.[51]

Raja Rammohun Roy thinks that all those ideas and beliefs in religion, which are not in tune with the principles of morality, human dignity and freedom, must be attributed as fabrications of the profounder of false religions. Only those practices should be accepted which are not in conflict with the essence of religion. Blind reliance on tradition would be against the principle of reason. He points out that, as God has endowed man with reason, intellect and understanding, he has to adopt such course of action by the practice of which he would make moral and spiritual progress. In the religious philosophy of Raja Rammohun Roy, man emerges as an entity that is capable of shaping his own destiny; man is a creation of God possessing God-like qualities, though nothing can be imagined as representing the attributes of God.

Roy does not support the views which hold that man is a sinful creature. That man is essentially good and that it is only the actions of man which make him a sinner or a saint. Man cannot be equated with God, for he will be judged by God according to his deeds. He envisages that religion makes it possible for man to return to the original source, wherein the individual finds unity with the Supreme.

Christianity

Raja Rammohun Roy's concern for the social implications of religious doctrines contributed significantly to his interest in the teachings of Jesus. As he wrote in introduction to *The Precepts of Jesus:*

---

51 *Tuhfat-ul-Muwahhiddin.* p, 11.

"This simple code of religion and immorality is so admirably calculated to elevate men's ideas to high and liberal notions of God ..... and is so well fitted to regulate the conduct of the human race in the discharge of their various duties to themselves, and to society, that I cannot but hope the best effects from its promulgation in the present form."[52]

It was also largely his concern for the social well-being of his countrymen which made him so relentless in his attack on polytheism and image worship resulted in the destruction of "every humane and social feeling."[53] He acknowledged that significant religious change needed to occur for the sake of his countrymen's "political advantage and social comfort." His campaign against *Satī* was a good example of his own determination to bring about such change. He also opposed polytheism and image worship. There seems to be ample evidence to support a growing number of scholars who have recently interpreted Raja Rammohun Roy primarily as a religious utilitarian whose central concern was the well-being of society. His social concern signaled a change from an emphasis of "mystery and metaphysics to ethics and philanthropy."[54] This change of emphasis which his work expresses so clearly is characteristic of a substantial amount of nineteenth century Indian thought.

Theology and metaphysics became tools of ethics and social change. Raja Rammohun Roy's contributions to modern Indian religious thought are diverse. Some of them, such as his emphasis on the *Upaniṣads* and *Brahma Sūtra*, are a continuing legacy maintained by the *Brahmo Samāj*. Others have been more diffuse in their impact; that is, it is difficult to determine

52 Robert D. Baird (ed), *Religion in modern India*, pp. 172-173.

53 Robert D. Baird (ed), *Religion in modern India*, p. 173.

54 Iqbal Sing, *Rammohun Roy*, p. 78.

what influence Roy's position has had on subsequent thinkers. Whether those continuities can be traced or not, several significant features of his religious thought can be noted in summary.

Raja Rammohun Roy could be a student of "comparative religion" without making one tradition normative for others. His arguments in support of the gṛhastha involvement in religious discussion, and his personal campaign of publication and debate, contributed to the individualization of religious authority.[55]

His utilitarian approach to religious thought and social practice challenged the established priority of salvation[*mokṣa*] over social order [*dharma*]. He wrote very little about salvation but a great deal about the social order. He shifted the focus of ethical discussion from asceticism to humanitarianism. He argued that the many regulations of food and drink were burdens which obscured people's ability to see and respond to the needs of other people.

Although Raja Rammohun Roy never systematically developed these aspects of his thought into a unified philosophy, it is worth noting that these features of his thought provide adequate premises for articulating a philosophy of a secular state.

---

55 Robert D. Baird, (ed), *Religion in modern India*, p. 174.

3

Swami Vivekananda

Vivekananda was born on 12 January 1863 in Calcutta, now Kolkata. His real name was Narendranath Datta.[56] His parents were Viswanath Datta and Buvanewswari. When he was in middle teens, he started going to college in Calcutta. He was a good looking athletic youth and extremely intelligent. He was also a fine singer and could play several musical instruments and also became proficient in swimming, riding and wrestling. He showed a great power for leadership among the boys of his own age. At that period, Calcutta was the chief port of entry for European ideas and cultural influences. No young Indian student could remain unaffected by them. Through the writings of the *Brahmo Samāj* leaders he was drawn towards India's religious and philosophical heritage, and familiarized with the Indian thought. He made good study of Indian scriptures as well as of Western thought.

In November 1881, for the first time he met Sri Ramakrishna Paramahansa and went to Dakshineswar with a divided mind—half of him eager for self dedication and devotion, the other western educated half, skeptical, impatience of superstition. He is initially unconvinced towards the teachings of Sri Ramakrishna, but after a brief period of doubt and psychological resistance, he surrendered himself completely to Ramakrishna's influence and accepted him as his guru. The main influence upon Vivekananda's thought is of Hindu philosophy, particularly of the *Vedānta*. Most of his thought

56 Swami Vidyatmananda, *What religion is*, XXIV.

is derived from the Hindu scriptures, the *Upaniṣads* and the *Vedānta*. His philosophy was greatly influenced by the understanding of religious and socio-economic conditions of the Indian people. Vivekananda always emphasized the need of re-interpreting *Vedānta* in accordance with the demands and needs of the time.

Vivekananda is impressed by the Buddhist assertion that the raft with the help of which one crosses a river in storm, should be left for the use of others. Buddha himself, even after attaining *nirvāṇa,* kept on roaming about helping others in their struggles against suffering. Vivekanada believes that man contains within him the spark of Divinity. He takes up the ideal of service and love from Christianity. He was also under the influence of the *Brahmo Samāj,* and it can be said that his strong feelings against the prevalent orthodox and superstitious rites were generated under that influence. The *Gītā's* stress on "selfless work" was also of constant inspiration to Vivekananda.

However, the deep influence, in the light of which every other influence was re-shaped, was that of his Guru, Sri Ramakrishna. It is said that Ramakrishna brought about a spiritual transformation in the personality and the mental make-up of Vivekananda. By the time of the demise of Sri Ramakrishna on 16 August 1886,[57] Vivekananda had already become the foremost among his disciples. He traversed the vast Indian land from the Himalayas to Kanyakumari.

Vivekananda participated in the World Parliament of Religions at Chicago in September 1893[58] to preach the spiritual wisdom of India. From that moment it has been said, Hinduism like her ancient 'step daughter', Buddhism, became a propagating religious philosophy.[59]

---

57 Swami Vedyatmananda, *What religion is,* XXIV.

58 Swami Vedyatmananda, *The complete works,* Vol. 1, p. 3.

59 Thomas Mannumel, S.J. *The advaita of Vivekananda,* p. 1.

In the Parliament of Religions, he gave an exposition of *Vedānta*. But when the sessions were over he resumed his role as the exponent of Ramakrishna's ideas which he was convinced, contained the essence of *Advaita Vedānta*. In May 1887, he founded the Ramakrishna Mission. The aim of the mission was the integration of educational, philanthropic and religious activities. A monastery, known as the Ramakrishna Math, was also established at Belur, near Calcutta. In June 1899, Vivekananda sailed for a second visit to the Western world. Swami Vivekananda died on 4 July 1902.

Vivekananda maintains that all the great prophets of the world religions are the incarnations of the Infinite. As a student of philosophy, the question of faith in God very much haunted his mind. He looked to persons who could say that they had seen God, but found none. He wanted to meet a person who could talk about God with the authority of personal experience of God. In 1881, he happened to meet Ramakrishna Paramahamsa and asked him straight away if he had seen God. He said he had, and if Naren so wished, he could even show God to him. His question was satisfactorily answered for the first time and from that moment he realized the fact that Ramakrishna was an extra-ordinary man. Ramakrishna had, from the very first meeting, found in Naren all those qualities, which were necessary to spread his message all over the world. Gradually he led him into the spiritual realm by easy stages and at last to the highest realm of inward experience. Three days before his death, he had handed over all his spiritual wealth to Naren and reminded him that he was born to accomplish great things in the world.

After the death of Ramakrishna on 16 August 1886, Naren took up the leadership of the great mission, which the master had assigned for him in his mind. He travelled all over India as a *Parivrājaka*, from Himalayas to Cape Comorin, in order to know the cultural, social and economic conditions of India.

He impressed the people by his way of life, genuine love and sympathy for all. Through it he obtained the direct experience of the misery of the downtrodden masses, dreadful social injustice, poverty and social backwardness of the people of India.

He realized the great truth that the poor must be ridden of their poverty otherwise it is futile to preach religion. He also realized the cultural, spiritual, traditional strength and assimilative power of India. The very outstanding mission in his life is to revitalize Hinduism, in other words *Sanātana dharma*, that is, the religion developed from the *Vedas* and the *Upaniṣads*. He considers the term 'Hinduism' in its universal sense, as a religion that leads mankind to the path of everlasting peace, love and freedom.

Hinduism is not a mere religion with superstitious practices. It is mainly concerned with certain fundamental spiritual laws for the righteous conduct of human beings in all spheres of activity. It, as a way of life, is the mother of all ways of life, a universal guideline for global life. Being conscious of the spiritual poverty of the West and the neglect of material factors by the East, his aim is to reveal the universality of Hinduism not only to the East but also to the whole mankind. It is clear when he declares: "I have a message to the West as Buddha had a message to the East." It is to bind the people together to exchange ideas and enrich their respective forms of culture with modern knowledge. The spiritual resurgence of the whole mankind is the scope of his message. Vivekananda founded the Ramakrishna Mutt and Mission in 1896 to preach the teaching of his Master Ramakrishna Paramahamsa. It was based on the dictum '*Ātmanomokṣārtham Jagaddhitayaca*', for the salvation of one's own soul and the welfare of the world.

The deep influence by his Master culminated in the spiritual transformation of his entire personality and marked out a turning point in his life. He describes this experience as follows: "The touch at once gave rise to a novel experience within me. With my eyes open I saw that the walls and everything in the room, whirled rapidly and vanished into naught, and the whole universe together with my individuality was about to merge in an all-encompassing mysterious void."

His central ideas spring from the influence of Ramakrishna Paramahamsa. In the words of Swami Nikhilananda: "It was his Master who taught him the divinity of the soul, the non-duality of the God-head, the unity of existence and one more thing—that is the universality or harmony of all religions." He was also influenced and inspired by the cultural and human values preserved in the scriptures of the three main religions, namely, Hinduism, Islam and Christianity. He emphasized the realization of human values as the central principle of all religions. His life and teaching may be described as a source of inspiration and stimulus for the contemporary modern thinkers like Mahatma Gandhi, Rabindranath Tagore, Jawaharlal Nehru and Dr. S. Radhakrishnan.

Though his teaching is essentially spiritualistic, its foundation, on the other hand, is rationalistic and realistic. His exhortation is categorical in nature. It is evident when he asserts: "Begin with disbelief. Analyze, test, prove everything, and then take it." There is no question of any blind belief, superstition and performance of rituals based on the authority of persons and scriptures. It is acceptable even to the modern scientific man. He examines the nature of reality or truth, God, nature and man in order to establish the harmonious relationship among them. He interprets facts both from the rational and suprarational levels of existence.

According to him, the divine-human relationship is mystical because it is the experience of the whole man with the whole Reality. It is a matter of an immediate experience or direct intuition into which he turns inwards and loses himself into the Reality, one individual self is as good as the endless universe as one can find the whole ocean in a drop. Vivekananda describes it as follows: "It is a vision, an inspiration, a plunge into the unknown and the unknowable, making the unknowable more than the known, for it can never be known". It is the transition of one's personality into the plane of the Universal Spirit. There is an element of mystic trance, which is universal in character in the religious urge of man, but the existence of this element does not make his religion unscientific because it is the root of all science.

His mission is to reconcile faith with reason by removing all irrational elements from religion. In the words of Romain Rolland: "He of all modern men achieved the highest equilibrium between the diverse force of thought, and was one of the first to sign a treaty of peace between the two forces eternally warning within us, the forces of reason and of faith." Being conscious of the attitude of the modern mind, he allows persons to use their reasoning faculties and conceive God in the light of their thinking.

According to Vivekananda, the word 'faith' in its true sense, means faith in oneself. It is the faith in the inherent infinite potentialities within man. This faith in oneself is considered the first essential pre-requisite for the faith in God. Here man understands the oneness of himself with the Universal Self. He declares as follows: "The great thing is to have faith in oneself, even before faith in God; but the difficulty seems to be that we are losing faith in ourselves day-by-day."

This faith in God is possible only with the realization of God within us or with the knowledge of the real Spirit. Wherever there is true faith, there is right knowledge, which enables one to zero the distance between man and man, man and nature, and finally even between God and man.

Indian Renaissance Movement

Bengal shared in the Indian Renaissance Movement during the latter half of the nineteenth century. A galaxy of great men like Raja Rammohun Roy, Keshab Chandra Sen, Dayananda Saraswati, Ramakrishna Paramahamsa and Swami Vivekananda made their presence felt during this period which is generally considered as the golden era in the history of India. The main objective of Indian Renaissance Movement was to face the challenge posed by the importation of Western ideas and values on Indian culture and social outlook. It revived and restored the lost individuality and reconstructed the faith in man regarding a secularized view of life. Indian Renaissance tried to modernize Hinduism by discarding the irrational rituals, false doctrines, and monopolistic priest-craft. The movement has a universal rather than a sectarian outlook.

The aim was to alleviate the whole of humanity from worldly miseries and the radical divine transformation of life. The pioneers of Indian Renaissance, who were greatly conscious of the social, political and religious degradation of Indian culture, understood the value of the glorious Indian tradition and its practical significance in daily life. Respecting the religious sentiments of the people, they declared that they were also not ready to reject the authority of the Hindu scriptures. They wanted to reinstate *Vedānta* in a correct way in the light of scientific knowledge and changed conditions, in order to achieve harmony between present and past and to fulfill the new requirements of the modern era.

Under the influence of western education, the modern religious thinkers became conscious of individual freedom and a sense of human dignity. Inspired by the new notions and values, both religious and secular, the pioneers of Indian Renaissance reacted against the social evils in life. After having read from classical Sanskrit texts, these people claimed that the practices in Hindu society were only interpolations and that they have no basis in the *Śāstras*. They spread a new message of renaissance in all spheres of life—in politics, religion, literature, education, industries and social reorganization, which created an awareness thus removing the darkness of the ages.

English education and scientific knowledge helped advance the process of social renaissance. Meanwhile the Christian missionaries went about with their humanitarian works for the welfare of the entire India, irrespective of caste, creed, age, sex and the economic or social status. They started educational institutions for girls as well as boys belonging to the already identified lower and untouchable castes. The rise of new renaissance caused a wave of reforming activities first in Bengal and then throughout the country. Swami Vivekananda's religious thought is rational and original. Let us analyze his approach towards major concepts of religious philosophy.

God

According to Vivekananda, the Reality is one Absolute *Brahman*. He says that Reality is one but not a 'whole'. The concept of a 'whole' implies that there must be parts, which when organized, give the whole. According to him, Absolute is perfect unity, and therefore the distinction between whole and parts completely vanishes. He says that the Absolute can be described as *Sat-Cit-Ānanda*. The concept of *Sat* (existence) and *Cit* (consciousness) are similar to the *Sat* and *Cit* of *Advaita Vedānta*, but the concept of *Ānanda* (bliss) has been greatly strengthened by Vivekananda under the influence of Buddhism and Christianity.

Vivekananda believes that the religious aspirations of man demand satisfaction, and that demand can be met only by a personal God. In Sankara's *Advaita Vedānta* also the concept of God has been given a place, but there God has been conceived as a product of ignorance and *Māyā*, and as such, is not real from the real point of view—the *Paramārthika dṛṣṭi;* but Vivekananda believes that Absolute and God are not two—that God is not a creation of *Māyā*. These distinctions surely arise on account of ignorance or our limited ways of apprehension, but knowledge means the realization of the irrelevance of such a distinction.

Metaphysically speaking, reality is absolute Brahman, the same reality viewed from the religious point of view is God. He, who is supremely real, is also the object of our devotion and worship. That is why, Vivekananda emphasizes the all-pervasive nature of God. God is present everywhere and in everything. Through his control the sky expands, through his control the air breathes, through his control the sun shines and through his control all live. He is the reality in nature. He is the soul of your soul. He says, "The Absolute is that ocean, while you and I, and sun and stars, and everything else are various waves of that ocean. And what makes the waves different? Only the form, and that form is time, space and causation all entirely dependent on the wave."[60]

World

Vivekananda conceives the cosmos almost in the Sankara's way. Sankara says that in reality there has never been any creation, from the transcendental point of view, creation, according to Sankara is unreal. It is true that he also comes to discuss the process of creation, but that has validity only from a lower, the empirical point of view.

Vivekananda not merely asserts the reality of the world. But feels that *Vedānta* does not intend to say that the world is unreal. He thinks that the word *Mithyā* has been misunderstood. There are many other scholars of *Vedānta* who also feel that way. They all feel that in *Vendānta* the word *Mithyā* has been used in a special sense. It means that which has no permanent value that which is constantly changing and varying—that which is transitory and temporary.

60 Swami Vivekananda, *The complete works, Vol. II*, p. 136.

Religion

Vivekananda says that the end of all religions is the realizing god in the soul.[61] He says if it be true that God is the centre of all religions,[62] religion is a necessity of life. Ordinarily only those things are regarded as necessary for life which satisfy the daily and the outer needs of life. Food, clothing, shelter, etc. are examples of what can be called, physical or materialistic needs. But, they are not the only needs of life. This is clearly proved from the fact that they alone do not fully satisfy man, even in the full of luxury, man wants something higher. This desire is his religious hunger, without seeing satisfaction for which he cannot live.

According to Vivekananda, the impersonal absolutism of Sankara, the *Bhakti mārga* of Ramanuja and his followers, and the humanism of the Buddha, these three elements have blended into each other and made India's religious consciousness. The only force which can bring about an enduring union between men of different cultures and persuasion is love. "The whole cosmos is a manifestation of love, from the lowest atom to the highest ideal. Love is the motive power of the universe. Under the impetus of love, Jesus Christ stands ready to give up his life for humanity, the Buddha even for an animal, without love the universe would fall to pieces in a moment. This love is god."

Vivekananda demonstrates in a number of ways how religion has to be regarded as a necessary aspect of life. Those who do not consider this as necessary do so because they identify religion with some of its expressions which appear to them as not necessary in any way. But, the fact that there is a longing of a higher kind—a longing for something that the physical environment cannot satisfy—so religion is a necessary aspect of life.

---

61 Swami Vivekananda, *The complete works, Vol. I*, p. 324.

62 Swami Vidyatmananda, *What religion is*, p. 25.

There appears to be an element of inevitability in religion, it cannot be given up. Trying to give up religion will itself become a religion. That also proves it necessary. The historical fact of the survival of religion itself is an evidence of its necessary character. Political or social organizations remain prominent for sometime, and then they pass out, but religions have continued to live through all circumstances even in adverse and hostile ones. Religion has never been vanquished. Whenever it appears that religion is being suppressed, it reappears in some form or the other. What can be a better demonstration than this of the fact that religion is a necessary aspect of life. Even religion has no right to claim a privileged position or to question reason in the field of knowledge. Religion may bring us special types of emotional experience. He wanted truth to be preached openly. According to Vivekananda, in every religion there are three parts[63]—Philosophy, Mythology and Ritual. Philosophy presents the whole scope of that religion setting forth its basic principles, the goals and the means for reaching it. Mythology consists of legends relating to the moral and spiritual adventures of men and supermen. Rituals are manner of performing Divine service.

Vivekananda maintains that there are immense and infinite potentialities in man. He calls the sum-total of these potentialities 'divinity' which is already in man. To awaken or manifest this divinity, this in-dwelling spirit is the be all and end-all of human life. This conception of man is based on the *Vedānta* which says that he himself is God (*so' ham*). Vivekananda says:

Nor angel I, nor man, nor brute,
Not body, mind, nor he or she,
The books do stop in wonder mute,
To tell my nature; I am He.[64]

---

63 Swami Vidyatmananda, *What religion is*, p. 25.

64 Swami Vivekananda, *The complete works, Vol. VIII*, p. 163.

Vivekananda applied "Sankara's idea that the *ātman* is in its essence the same as the *Brahman*; he thus shower the inner greatness and divinity of man and taught people that service to man is essentially the same as service to god (*Brahman*)."[65]

Swami Vivekananda introduced the social service as part of the monastic discipline. "Vivekananda introduced the idea of social service for the monks in an organized form. This was an important change in the social relationships between the monasteries."[66] He believed that it was an insult to offer sermons instead of food to a hungry man. Before religion could be taught to the masses, they required to be fed, clothed and educated. "May I be born again and again", Vivekananda says "and suffer thousands of miseries, so that I may worship the only God that exists, the only God I believe in, the sum total of all souls—and above all, my God the miserable, my God the poor of all races, of all species, is the special object of my worship."

According to Vivekananda, services of humanity is service to divinity. He preached his famous doctrine of *Daridra Nārāyaṇa Seva*—the doctrine of worshipping the Nārāyaṇa in the poor. He advises every man each day to take hungry Nārāyaṇa or a lame Nārāyaṇa or a blind Nārāyaṇa, six or twelve, according to his means, to feed him, to offer him the same worship as he would to Śiva or Viṣṇu in the temple. Thus it is not mere social service but service of man as worship of God. This doctrine of worshipping Nārāyaṇa in the poor, according to Vivekananda, is doubly advantageous. The people whom we serve are benefited by our service but the benefit accruing to us is a hundred times more than the people serve. For, by serving others get citta-śuddhi, self-purification which is the aim of human life. Realization comes through such purification. So we must be thankful to the poor people for they give us the

65 Raju, P.T. *The philosophical traditions of India*, p. 230.

66 *Ibid.*

opportunity of attaining self-purification. In the words of Vivekananda: "What is needed is citta-śuddhi, purification of the heart. And how does that come? The first of all worship is the worship of the *Virāṭ*-of those all around us."

Vivekananda, therefore, points out that the gist of all worship is to be pure (to be good) and to do good to others. He who sees Śiva in the poor, in the weak and in the diseased really worships Śiva and if he sees Śiva only in images, his worship is but preliminary. He, who has served one poor man seeing Śiva in him, pleases the Śiva more than the man who sees only in temples. From this we derive the idea that the fundamental religion consists in 'being good' and 'doing good.' Doing good is as important as being good. Being good means approximating God. And that is self purification or renunciation. Doing good means the continuation of being good. And it is only by being good that doing well becomes possible; that is genuine renunciation must precede true service.

Universal Religion

Swami Vivekananda says that a simple insight into the natures of different religions will show that they are not actually contradictory to each other. He says in one sense, religion is universal; the particularities, dogmas, doctrines and religious ceremonies only help religion, but the essence of religion itself consists in God–realization. The realization of universal religion, according to Vivekananda, would enable different sects and religions to reconcile their loyalty to their respective churches with a genuine spirit of unbounded Catholicism towards all other faiths. Different religions emphasize different qualities of religion and, as such, it is not possible to find the common elements. Islam, for example, lays emphasis on universal brotherhood, Hinduism on spirituality, Christianity on self-purification for entering into the Kingdom of God. It is difficult to compare these and, therefore, the tenants of universal religion would not be the common characters of different religions. Vivekananda is not dismayed by this because he recognized the natural necessity of variation. The elements of universal religion would consist in recognizing that there may be various and different ways of approach to the religious objectives. It gives perfect liberty to the individual in this regard. But, at the same time, the spirit of universal religion demands that every approach must be large-hearted enough to have a respect for the other ones.

The one watch-word for universal religion, according to him, is acceptance. Acceptance is not just tolerance. Tolerance is negative in its import, it implies, at least at times that something is being allowed in spite of its being wrong. He recommends positive acceptance. That is why, he says that he can worship in any form with any individual or sect. He says that he can enter and offer his prayers anywhere, in temple, or a church, or a mosque, or any other place. The believer in the universal religion has to be broad-minded and open-hearted, he would be prepared to learn from the scriptures of all religions, and keep his heart open for what may come in the future.

Religion, properly understood, is nothing if it is not universal, and our search for a world-religion should be directed to find out the essence of religion itself which, when discovered, will reveal itself to be the one universal religion. "Therefore," says Vivekananda, "religious ideas will have to become universal, vast and infinite and then alone we shall have the fullest play of religion ...[67] What is needed is fellow-feeling between the different types of religion, seeing that they all stand or fall together, a fellow-feeling which springs from mutual esteem and mutual respect. If there is to be a universal religion, it must be the religion that identifies itself with the realization of God in the soul. That is the one universal religion. If there is one universal truth in all religions, I place it here—

67 Swami Vivekananda. *The complete works, Vol. II*, p. 68.

in realizing God. Ideals and methods may differ, but that is the central point. There may be a thousand different radii, but they all converge to the one centre, and that is the realization of God."[68]

Such an attitude enables Vivekananda to discover at least one such element which can be said to be common to all religions in a general way, and which consequently may represent the essence of universal religion. That common point is God. Even things that are apparently different may be similar in a particular sense.

Man and woman are different, but as human beings they are alike. As living beings, men, animals and plants are all one. In that way, although different religions talk of different aspects of the Truth, as aspects of the same Truth, they are all one. It is true that sometimes we may have different ideas in the religious doctrines of different faiths; yet they may all belong to the same great universal truth. They are not in error. "It is the journey from truth to truth, lower truth to higher truth."[69] Vivekananda points out that if a man journeying towards the sun, takes a photograph of the sun at every stage as he advances, he will find that no two photographs of the sun are alike; and yet it cannot be denied that they are all photographs of the same sun.[70] Similarly, the different religions give different descriptions of Reality from different points of view. But they are all descriptions of the same Reality and are equally true. They are all different roads leading to the same centre—God.[71] He says, "I want to propagate a religion that will be equally acceptable to all minds; it must be equally philosophic, equally emotional, equally mystic, and equally conducive to action."[72]

---

68 Swami Vivekananda, *The complete works, Vol. I*, pp. 324-325.

69 Swami Vivekananda, *The complete works, Vol. II*, p. 327.

70 *Ibid.*, p. 366.

71 Robert D.Baird (ed), *Religion in modern India*, Vol. V, p. 292.

72 Robert D.Baird (ed), *Religion in modern India*, Vol. II, p. 387.

In this way he emphasizes the need to recognize the value of all the paths, in order to satisfy and serve the needs of different aspirants and different temperaments. Such is the concept of universal religion taught by Vivekananda. He declares that his religion is the search after the Truth. It is beyond the sacred scriptures like the *Vedas*, the *Bible*, and the *Quran*, the spiritual revelations to the world. These scriptures are written in human languages, which are inadequate to express the super sensuous experience. They describe certain spiritual truth, but not the whole Truth, which transcends human comprehension. In the words of Vivekananda: "The *Bible*, the *Vedas*, the *Quran*, and all other sacred books are but so many pages, and an infinite number of pages remain yet to be unfolded". The founders, prophets and messengers of all the religions of the world declared that they had an experience of the super sensuous state. The realization of this super sensuous experience is the basis of every religion. The nature of such experience is trans-empirical and trans-rational.

The oration of Vivekananda on the world scenario at the Parliamanent of Religions in Chicago in 1893 may be considered as a great turn as it marked out the turning point not only of inter-religious understanding and universal brotherhood, but also the proper understanding of the true spirit of religions. It also signified the death-knell of fanaticism, bigotry and sectarianism of all kinds in the name of religion. *The New York Herald* spoke of Vivekananda as follows: "He is undoubtedly the greatest figure in the Parliament of Religions. After hearing him we feel how foolish it is to send missionaries to this learned nation."[73]

Almost all world religions were represented and their respective religious leaders had arrived fully prepared to establish their own credentials and supremacy of their faith and beliefs. The universal religion of Vivekananda is really

---

73 Swami Vivekananda, *Chicago address*, p. 62.

a call for unity among the great religions. It is not only the synthesis of the elements taken from all the religions of the world, but also the realization of the fact that religions of the world preach the same Truth in different ways. The different religions of the world are different pathways to the common spiritual goal. They are like the pearls strung harmoniously upon God's necklace. The passage cited by Sister Nivedita in this context is significant: "All these are threaded upon me, as pearls upon a string."[74] It indicates that there is an underlying thread of unity in the form of God that is running through all these religions. Realization of this fact is essential for the smooth running of great religions.

Despite his universal spiritual outlook, he was a humanist in its true sense. His message is not against the material development of man. But it gives mankind a warning against the threat of excessive materialism. Opposition to material surfeit does not mean neglecting the improvement of the basic needs of man's life. Such advancement is necessary for the physical and mental development of man, which is an essential preparation for the spiritual evolution. Here we must remember the great *Śarīram kalu dharma sadanam*. None can practically see a picture without a canvas behind it, nor can a man achieve in his spiritual perfection without the existence of his body. Vivekananda sternly supports this basic truth. He even crossed the ocean with the hope of getting material aid for the poor and downtrodden brothers and sisters.

The gospel of Vivekananda pictures the infinite spiritual dimension of the true nature of man's spirit as divine. Human birth is considered as precious privilege attained because of good deeds performed in several births. All these good deeds comprise the universal good deed. In other words, all these births are due to the spiritual division of labour. It is of great significance as it marks a turning point in the long process

74 Sister Nivedita, *The master as I saw him*, p. 5.

of transmigration that every soul undergoes. This world of action provides man the greatest and the finest opportunity to become perfect. Every moment of his life is a new opening to the ultimate of timeless freedom. He declares as follows:

> "The man form is higher than even the angel form, and of all forms it is the highest; man is the highest being in creation, because he attains freedom."[75]

Man is conscious of his superior status and of the greater possibilities of spiritual progress. Every individual, however degraded and fallen he might be, is capable of growing infinitely. He never becomes absolutely imperfect or absolutely perfect. He always keeps tending towards perfection. The essence of man is non-finite spirit. In the words of Vivekananda. "A brute is like the diamond in the dirt and dust-brush, the dust off and it is a diamond, just as pure as polished diamond if the dust had never been on it, and we must admit that every soul is a crude diamond."[76]

Religion is the realization of the spark of diviners in man as eternal, everlasting and pure. It teaches mind not only to refrain from the evil but also to insist on doing well to others. It brings man near to the supremacy of God. Vivekananda describes the task of religion as follows: "Religion is the idea which is raising the brute unto man, and man unto God."[77]

If the spirit in man that forces him to go beyond his animal nature and to behave like a real man, he is considered as the crown of creation and has the privilege of realizing God immanent in him. He asserts as follows: Rise, thou effulgent one, rise thou who art always pure, rise thou birthless and deathless, rise almighty and manifest thy true nature. It implies the demand to listen to the call of divine in man.

---

75 Swami Vivekananda, *Complete works, Vol. II* p. 258.

76 Swami Vivekananda, *Complete works, Vol. V,* p. 409.

77 *Ibid.,* Vol-V, p. 409.

The source of infinite strength and fearlessness is the other principle feature in his teachings. He considers goodness is strength and sin is weakness. Strength is the only source of true religion. Thus the soul, saved from the bondage of fear, is attained only by a fearless soul. Freedom from all kinds of external and internal enemies by which calmness and ineffable peace of mind are provided. The positivistic and constructive force of his teaching is evident in his own words: "Arise, Awake! Awake from this hypnotism of weakness. None is really weak; the soul is infinite, omnipotent and omniscient. Stand up, assert yourself, proclaim the God within you, do not deny Him."[78] The living faith in God within man is the only significant step towards the acquisition of fearlessness, boundless energy is permeated by the power of his teaching in which the illumination of one's own consciousness empowering man with a new view of life in a greatly unified and glorious world.

Vedānta in Modern Age

The practical teaching of the *Vedānta* occupies the key position in Vivekananda's mission in which universal religion is the centre point with all its modern, scientific approach. Its simplicity is acceptable even by the modern science. Being rational, scientific and practical, it is capable of satisfying the demand of the modern science in regard to the widest generalization that everything is self-explainable. In this connection, *Brahman* is such a concept that has everything with him and nothing without. The *Taittirīya Upaniṣad* makes it clear that everything comes from *Brahman*, lives in *Brahman* and dies into *Brahman* to repeat the same again. Every religion accepts this phenomenon just as "Jehova" of Jews and "Allah" of Muslims, etc. The dogmatic beliefs yielding no place to reason began vanishing by the virtue of his teachings with reason.

---

78 Swami Vivekananda, *Complete works, Vol.* II, p. 193.

The fundamental truth of *Vedānta* is to become the part of the daily experience of our life. The truth of *Vedānta* extends its verification among saints and sages, monarchs and common people, etc., quite equally with common importance in a liberation of their own soul. The liberated souls render very much to the spiritual perfection and liberation of many other souls. The greatness of *Vendānta* is its universality.

Yoga provides for everybody salvation quite equally. Everyone of us has the possibility to experience the truth, which is the ultimate explanation of everything. He declares as follows: "These prophets were not unique; they were men as you or they were great *yogis*. They had gained this superconsciousness and you and I can get the same. They were not peculiar people. The very fact that one man reached that state proves that it is possible for every man to do so. Not only it is possible, but every man must, eventually, get to that state, and that is religion."[79]

Vedānta projects the similarities among the religions of the world and renders to the harmony among them. His religion is universal, for it takes in all the religions. There will be no distinction of the world in the name of the caste, creed or religion. The universal message of Vivekananda's aim is to remove hatred, violence, suspicion and prejudice among the people.

The aim of the universal religion of Vivekananda is to establish love, peace, religious tolerance, co-operation and goodwill among nations. It throws light on the universal eternal truths embodied in all the great religions of the world, which comprise an everlasting unity. Realization of the need of harmonizing the essence of *Vedas*, the *Bible* and the *Quran* is acceptable to all people irrespective of differences in race, religion, language, customs and traditions. In the religion of *Vedānta*, the Hindu, the Muslim and the Christian are all one by

---

79 Swami Vivekananda, *Complete works, Vol. I*, p. 185.

being the children of the Almighty God. His teaching has the power to bridge the barriers of fanaticism and exclusiveness into a communion of universal brotherhood.

Theism

According to Vivekananda, the idea of personal God in theism is a very convenient, natural, common-sense explanation of the universe. But it is not a true scientific generalization. First of all, the acceptance of a personal God as the all-knowing, all merciful, all good and all just is not consistent with the problem of good and evil in human experience. Secondly, the superstitions and tyranny in the name of religion lead him to the conclusion that such a God cannot be true. He finds solution to all the problems of human existence in the idea of the Absolute, which is the unifying ground of everything in the universe. He employs the analogy of a geometrical circle.

> "The nearer we are to the centre of a circle, the nearer we are to the common ground in which all the radii meet; and the farther we are from the centre, the more divergent is our radial line from the others."[80]

The centre where all the radii of existence meet is inside, that is in the innermost core of the human soul, which is the centre of the whole universe. Human life is worthless if man ceases to push forward in his inquiry into that which is beyond and behind the material world. It is clear when Vivekananda says, "If man rests content with the present and gives up all search into the beyond, mankind will have to go back to the animal plane again."

As a rationalist, he finds in pure *Advaita* the God of a scientific and rationalistic religion. Like Sankara, he accepts *Brahman* as *nirguṇa* and *nirākāra* in its eternal aspect as the Absolute. The Impersonal Absolute in its sportive aspect when involved in the process of creation, preservation and destruction, he calls

80 Swami Vivekananda, *Complete works, Vol. III*, p. 157.

the personal God. There is no fundamental difference between the Impersonal Absolute and the personal God (*nirākāra* and *sākāra*). The idea of personal God is only the manifestation of the Impersonal Absolute. One is not more real than the other. Rather it indicates that they are infinite dimensions to the manifestation of Reality. As a result, there may be a variety of approaches to Reality. Vivekananda says,

> "You and I, as representing ideas, have grown, these gods also, as representing ideas, have grown. This may seem somewhat curious to you–that God can grow. He cannot. He is unchangeable. But man's idea of God are constantly changing and expanding."[81].

He believes in the evolution of the idea of God from the primitive and anthropomorphic level to the higher Impersonal Absolute. The personal God is called the Impersonal Absolute when viewed without any reference to cosmos or creation of the world.

According to Vivekananda, Advaita *Vedānta* does not in reality denounce the sense-world and all that is finite as absolutely unreal. But it merely emphasizes that the world cannot have any fixed or absolute existence of its own. The *Iśā Upaniṣad* begins with a description of secret depths of the Truth: "Isavasyam idam sarvam, Yat kimca jagatyam jagat."[82] The meaning is that the whole universe with all its changing phenomena is filled with the spirit of God.

What Neo-*Vedānta* seeks to teach is the defecation of the world—giving up the world as it appears to the senses—and to know what it really is? Vivekananda declares that the whole world is God itself, which signifies the idea of spiritual harmony of all existence. The whole universe—heavens, planets, gods, living and non-living objects—is nothing but the expression of the Almighty God. Vivekananda, says:

81 Swami Vivekananda, *Complete Works Vol. II*, p. 107.

82 Isa *Upanishad*, 1.1.

> "The sum total of this whole universe is God himself. Is God then matter? No, certainly not, for matter is that God perceived by the five senses; that God as perceived through the intellect is mind; and when the spirit sees, he is seen as spirit. He is not matter, but whatever is real in matter is He."[83]

All things are the different manifestations of the same Reality. The same divine nature is present in the lowest worms as well as in the highest beings. The difference is only in manifestation. The world changes at every moment. But there is something that persists which our reason cannot grasp and yet is a fact. God is the immanent innermost principle underlying the world of manifestations. Vivekananda describes Him as follows:

> "He is the Great Poet, the Ancient Poet; the whole universe is His poem, coming in verses and rhymes and rhythms, written in infinite bliss."[84]

If every thing is God, then the world is not outside of God. According to him, God is both the material and efficient cause of this world. As Neo-*Vedāntins*, Vivekananda did not like to differentiate the sacred life from the secular affairs. His multifaceted powerful personality cannot be measured by any rigid classification. For him, religion is the search for the unity and identity behind the multiplicity and duality in the universe. It is the effort to realize harmony in all spheres of life.

Religion and Science

According to Vivekananda, religion is a quest for truth in practice. The whole effort of religion is to realize the presence of Truth by transcending the limitations of the senses and the reason. Religion is super sensuous knowledge. But the foundation of it is science and hence here is scope for both

---

83 Swami Vivekananda, *Complete works, Vol. I*, p. 375.

84 Ibid., II, p. 149.

the material and social advancement. There is no essential distinction between true science and true religion. The aim of all science is to find the truth, the one out of which every thing else can be manufactured. All truths flow from the same fountainhead, and when properly understood, must harmonize with one another. Religion is science in its incomplete and improper form. Science is religion in limitation, for it eliminates the spirit that gives value to nature. It is religion only when it becomes all comprehensive, universal and infinite in its outlook.

Modern science has also proved that the world processes as the manifestation of One Primordial Energy in a balanced manner. The scientific pursuit of empirical truth is not antagonistic to the religious pursuit of metaphysical truth. Religion has to transcend the sphere of empirical truth to experience the non-empirical metaphysical truth. It is man's ceaseless struggle to rise above the bond of nature and to become free.

Work and Worship

Work and worship are not exclusive of each other. The essence of work is worship itself. Vivekananda identifies the spirit of work with the spirit of worship. Here, work becomes a method of worshipping the world and everything in it as God. His religion is the outcome of the harmonious combination of the two ideals of life, the ideal of work and renunciation. It is not mere renunciation, but the renunciation of the work as it appears to the senses. Work without renunciation becomes completely fruitless. It is not the work, but the spirit in which it is done that binds individual consciousness. Work with the spirit of renunciation leads to self-realization. There is no distinction between sacred and secular, work and worship and life and religion.

The whole of nature is worship of God. Doing well to others is a means for revealing one's own Self or *Ātman*. He insists to worship God in poor as a way for God–realization. Self-sacrifice is the first requisite in the performance of selfless service. The desireless service to the poor is considered as the best form of worship. Romain Rolland claims as follows: "To see Śiva represented in living men and especially in the poor."[85] Religion is service to the poor and sacrifice even at the cost of one's own life for the benefit of others. The object of worship is man, the only existing God on the earth. Vivekananda says, "May I born again and again and suffer thousands of miseries, so that I may worship the only God that exists, the only God I believe in, the sum total of all souls–and above all, my God the wicked, my God the miserable, my God the poor of all races, of all species, is the special object of my worship". This is the most practical form of all worship. It channelizes its power into a new dimension of social service by providing a spiritual reality as a trait of social behaviour. It provides a spiritual background to the humanitarian ideals of compassion and charity by the service to the living God dwelling in the heart of all human beings.

Spirituality

The core of the universal religion of Vivekananda is spirituality. Everything in the universe including man is essentially spiritual. The realization of the spirit in its true nature is spirituality and the practical manifestation of this spirituality is religion. The more spiritual a man, the more universal he is. The test of spirituality is the ability to experience the Unity of Existence. The same spirit resides in the Christians, Hindus, Mohammedans and all others. His religion stands for the spiritualization of the whole mankind, which ultimately leads to the peace, and unity of all religions.

The backbone of progress—social, political, scientific and technological—is religion, the manifestation of the divine spirit within man. Religion is spirituality and it is complementary

85 Romain Rolland, *The life of Vivekananda and the universal gospel*, p. 102.

and contributory to the human development. It seeks to realize God in the soul of all human beings. Vivekananda says, "God is the Soul of our Souls, the Reality in us."[86] The role of true religion, that is spirituality, is to awaken this awareness in man.

Religions like Hinduism and Christianity admit a spirit element within man and its inseparable religion with God. Hinduism emphasizes the intimacy of Spirit more intensively than other religions. In the words of Radhakrishnan:

> "True religion is born of its spirit, not of flesh and blood, not of codes and customs, not of races and nations."[87]

The statement *Tatvam Asi* signifies the truth that this Supreme Spirit is in the soul of man. The statement of Jesus Christ "Kingdom of God is within you"[88] expresses the realization of the Spirit, a living reality in the experience of people. The word 'Islam' itself means the surrender of the soul or spirit within man to the will of the Omniscient, the Omnipotent and the most Merciful God. Religions are serviceable only in so far as they are spiritual in nature.

The religion of Vivekananda is universal in its scope. It seeks to see the universal and all pervading spirit of Truth in all the human beings. It eliminates every type of discrimination between man and man, man and nature, man and God, between one form of manifestation and the other form of manifestation. It has no geographical barriers. This is evident in the words of the Swami:

> "If there is ever to be a universal religion, it must be one which will have on location in place or time; which will be infinite like the God it will preach, and whose sun will shine upon the followers of Kṛṣṇa and

---

86 Swami Vivekananda, *Complete works, Vol. I,* p. 356.

87 Radhakrishnan and Muirhead (ed), *Contemporary Indian philosophy,* p. 502.

88 *Holy Bible, New Testament, Luke* 17:.21.

> Christ, on saints and sinners alike; which will not be Brahmanic or Buddhistic, Christian or Mohammedan, but the sum total of all these, and still have infinite space for development ... It will be a religion which will have no place for persecution or intolerance in its polity, which will recognize divinity in every man and woman, and whose whole scope, whose whole force, will be created in aiding humanity to realize its own true, divine nature."[89]

The gospel of universal religion is based on the realization of the essential truth underlying the teachings of the saints and prophets of different religions. The sense of fundamental unity is provided by the universal acceptance and religious tolerance of all other religions. Religious harmony means tolerance, acceptance and inclusion; but not exclusion. The interpretations of essence of *Vedas*, the *Bible*, the *Quran* and all the religions of the world are different. There should be a spirit of give and take. He further states that he has no difficulty in entering and offering his prayers anywhere, in a temple, or a church, or a mosque, or any other place. In the words of Vivekananda:

> "The Christian is not to become a Hindu or a Buddhist, nor a Hindu or a Buddhist to become a Christian. But each must assimilate the spirit of the others and yet preserve his individuality and grow according to his own law of growth."[90]

It is evident from Vivekananda's declaration "I shall go to the mosque of the Mohammedan; I shall enter the Christian's church and kneel before the crucifix; I shall enter the Budhistic temple, where I shall take refuge in Buddha and his law. I shall go into the forest and sit down in meditation with the Hindu. Not only shall I do all these, but I shall keep my heart open for

---

89 Swami Vivekananda, *Complete works, Vol. I*, p. 19.

90 *Ibid.*, p.24.

all that may come in the future."[91] The ideal of universal religion is spiritual rather than material. It is not an unattainable other worldly one. Vivekananda advocates practical methods to experience oneness in every form of life. In his own words:

> "Take up one idea. Make that one idea your life, think of it, dream of it, live of that idea. Let the brain, muscles, nerves, every part of your body, be full of that idea, and just leave every other idea alone."[92]

He states that one can choose the method he likes, and follow it with sincerity and earnestness; he will be able to reach the goal. This is the only way to attain success, and reach God through the one idea of one's choice. All religions of the world preach the same truth, but through different religious practices. Religions are different in beliefs, attitudes and practices, but they are one in essence. It indicates the unity in diversity of the universe. The different religions are the various expressions of the One Eternal Religion and are merely the different stages of the spiritual growth. Different rivers originate from different sources and merge in the same ocean. Once they merge into the ocean they loose their names and forms; in the same way all the religious paths lead to the same goal. In the words of Vivekananda:

> "As so many rivers, having their source in different mountains, roll down, crooked or straight, and at last come into the ocean—so, all these various creeds and religions, taking their start from different standpoints and running through crooked or straight courses, at last come unto thee."[93]

91 Swami Vivekananda, *Complete works, Vol.* II, p. 374.

92 *Ibid.*, I, p. 177.

93 Swami Vivekananda, *Complete works, Vol. II*, p. 390.

Mysticism

Mysticism is a natural element of Hinduism, whereas it is a relatively new concept to Islam. The mystic saints, the Sufis renounced pleasures, despised riches and honours and devoted themselves to a life of devotion and seclusion. Though there are minor differences, all saints in different religions agree in one respect and declare in one voice that unity underlies diversity. This is the basic characteristic of mysticism, the Unity or Oneness of all things. The mystic experience is the very centre of their being; it is the flame, which enlightens their whole life. The prophetic religions like Judaism, Christianity and Islam maintain that this Truth is essentially unknowable and it can be known only through their prophets.

Neti Neti description of *Brahman* in the *Upaniṣads* also points out the same fact that it is essentially unknowable and indescribable. The nature of this ultimate truth is mystical and hence cannot be fully described in rational language. In this mystic state, the *Jñāni* experiences nothing but the quality-less *Brahman*. Even when he comes out of his *Samādhi* the mystic sees everything as permeated by *Brahman*; he sees *Brahman* as the Self or *Ātman* of all beings; he perceives God everywhere and in everything and this is expressed in the *Mahāvākya Sarvam-khalu-idam-Brahma*.

Religion and Love

Love is the foundation of all religion. Universal religion of Vivekananda is the embodiment of pure love, which is the outcome of the realization of the oneness of humanity. Unselfish love has a power. It does not seek any return for love. Vivekananda says:

> "It is love without thought of return, love like that of the moth for the light."[94]

94 Swami Vivekananda, *Complete works, Vol. II*, p. 9.

He identifies love with truth for love is that unites the individual consciousness with the divine cosmic consciousness. The basis for the entire cosmic creation is love itself. Later on, this love transforms into selfless service and the selfless service into worship. Vivekananda declares:

> "It is in love that religion exists and not in ceremony, in the pure and sincere love in the heart. Unless a man is pure in body and mind, his coming into a temple and worshipping Śiva is useless."[95]

Jesus Christ identifies God with love and follows the same Rule of Love. He manifests his love and mercy to all men both good and bad, without regard to need of merit. That love is technically called as 'Agape'.[96] It can be realized only when one attains the ability to overcome anger by loving even his enemy. His love is unconditional since he does not expect anything in return. It is divine, noble and motiveless.

The central purpose of universal religion is service to humanity. Its principles refer to the unity and upliftment of the entire mankind. The people belonging to different faiths, cultures, races and traditions constitute the family of God. For Vivekananda, religion is not mere social service but service of the poor as worship of God. The gist of worship consists in being good and doing well for others. Social charity and service to the poor are natural expressions of love in action. In Christianity Jesus Christ insists:

> "To feed the hungry, to clothe the naked, to welcome the stranger, to cheer the sick, to visit the imprisoned—in short to love and serve man is to love and serve the Father."[97]

---

95 Swami Vivekananda, *Complete works, Vol.* III, p. 141.

96 *Holy Bible, New Testament, 1 Corinthians XI. 'Agape'-love or charity feast celebrated among the early Christians.*

97 *Holy Bible, New Testament, Mathew,* 25:24-46.

Hospitals, nursing homes, dispensaries, homes for the aged, destitute and orphanages and a number of other specialized institutions for the service of the weak and ailing members of the society are the expressions of love for all men. The aim of Hinduism is general good of whole mankind, *Sarvalokahita ratah* and *lokasaṃgraha*. In Islam, there is *Zakat* and *Sadaq* through which a Muslim discharges his duty to the poor and needy. *Zakat* is a monetary obligation. Every Muslim who possesses more than a minimum amount of wealth has to contribute at least a certain percentage of his total wealth for the society. It is not merely a charity; it is religious right, which the rich owe to the needy and poor, and to the society at large.

The universal religion of Vivekananda harmonizes all religions into one. Religious unity does not mean to achieve the external uniformity of religious conduct for social purposes, but a harmonious blending of religious variety into a symphony of spiritual quest. In the words of Romain Rolland, "Vivekananda wanted India to have an Islamic body and *Vedāntic* heart"[98] with reference to Hindu-Muslim difference; he states that the ideal society for India would be a union of the two great religions, Hinduism and Islam.

98 Romain Rolland, *The life of Vivekananda and the universal gospel*, p. 110.

4

Mahatma Gandhi

Mohandas Karamchand Gandhi, popularly known as Mahatma Gandhi, was born on 2 October 1869 at Porbandar in Gujarat, into a family which had served as ministers to one of the princely states that dotted that region.[99] His father Karamchand Gandhi was a member of the Rajasthan Court. He was for sometime Prime Minister in Rajkot and then in Vankaner. His father did not have any ambition to accumulate riches and left for them very little property. He grew up in an orthodox and deeply religious family, his mother Putlibai was deeply religious, particularly a fervent Vaiṣṇavite, given to many prayers, long fasts and frequent visits to the family shrine. She had strong common sense and well informed about all matters of State, and ladies of the court thought highly of her intelligence.

At the age of seven, Gandhi was put into a primary school in Rajkot where his family lived for a long time and after that he went to the suburban school and thence to the high school at the age of twelve years.

Gandhi said, "My books and my lessons were my sole companions."[100] He was married to Kasturbai at the age of thirteen[101] which made him, in later life, a severe critic of child marriage. Gandhi said in his autobiography that he was married, but not betrothed.

---

99 Aravind Sharma, *Modern Hindu thought*, p. 249.

100 M.K. Gandhi, *An autobiography*, p. 5.

101 R. De Smet and J.Neuner, p. 375.

> "Betrothal is a preliminary promise on the part of the parents of the boy and the girl to join them in marriage, and it is not inviolable.[102]

And five years later, in the year 1888, he matriculated and left for further studies in England. At first in England, he tried to lead a westernized way of life but very soon he gave up the idea and remained as an Indian because he had promised to his mother and elders of his caste to abstain from wine, meat and women, during his stay abroad.

Gandhi used to read all the 'holy books'—the *Bible*, the *Quran*, the *Bhagavad Gītā* and the *Dhammapada*—whatever it was, all the same to him. Gandhi said "I am a Hindu, I am a Moslem, I am a Jew, and I am a Christian. I am a Buddhist!" It was all the same to him. Part of the inspiration for this policy came from the Russian writer Leo Tolstoy, whose influence on Gandhi was profound.

> "South Africa turned out to be a mini-laboratory for Gandhi for his political and moral experiments, which he was to try out on a grander scale in India. It was here that he perfected the technique of *Satyāgraha* or non-violent resistance. The word means holding on to truth and Gandhi preferred it to the earlier term 'passive resistance', which he found misleading."[103]

The influences on Gandhi are varied and rich. D.K. Dutta classifies them mainly into three; (1) The Indian Influence, (2) The Western Influences, (3) Persian and Islamic Influences.[104]

---

102 M.K. Gandhi, *An autobiography*, p. 7.

103 Arabind Sharma, *Modern Hindu thought*, p. 252.

104 D.K. Dutta, *Social, moral and religious philosophy of Mahatma Gandhi–A critical analysis*, p. 25.

The Indian Influence

Gandhi learnt much from his mother Putlibai who was a deeply religious lady and his father Karamchand Gandhi and family's nurse Rambha who inculcated the idea of reciting the name of Rāma in the moments of difficulty. Gandhi said:

> "I think it is due to the seed sown by that good woman Rambha that today *Rāmanāma* is an infallible remedy for me."[105]

The family surroundings influenced his religious temperament and the religious needs. Gandhi learnt even from ordinary people, nurse, sweeper, servants, etc. In school days, he had formed the habit of speaking truth to everybody. He was quite opposed to telling a lie to anybody whether a teacher or a classmate. To tell a lie was considered by him as an irreligious act and breach of truth.[106]

Gandhi read *Shravana Pitribhakti Naatak* with great interest. He also saw the picture of Shravana carrying his blind parents on a pilgrimage. He said: "This book and the picture left an indelible impression on my mind."[107] The story of Hariścandra also influenced him.

Jainism is a living force in Gujarat, than in any other part of India. He read the life of Mahāvīra and also *Saddarasana Samuccaya,* the philosophical text of Haribhadra Suri. Jainism's theory of non-violence impressed him very much. Gandhi also read Edwin Arnold's, *The Light of Asia,* a famous book on the life of Lord Buddha. He said, "I owe a great deal to the inspiration that I have derived from the life of the enlightened one"[108]. Of the books that moulded him, *Gītā* can be ranked

105 M.K. Gandhi, *My religion,* p. 6.

106 M.K. Gandhi, *An autobiography,* p. 3.

107 M.K. Gandhi, *My teligion,* p. 4.

108 M.K. Gandhi, *All religions true,* p. 136.

first. The teachings of the *Gītā*, especially *Śloka* 62 and *Śloka* 63 of chapter 2, impressed him most and the book proved for him to be of priceless worth. He writes:

> "The verses in the second chapter made a deep impression on my mind, and they still ring in my ears. The impression has ever since been growing on me with the result that I regard it today as the book par excellence for the knowledge of truth. It has afforded me invaluable help in my moments of gloom."[109]

Gandhi said, "When doubt haunts me .... And when I see not one ray of light on the horizon, in *Bhagavad Gītā*, I find a verse to comfort me."[110] He also read *Mahābhārata* of Vyāsa, *Manu Smṛti*, *Upaniṣads*, and Patanjali's *Yoga Sūtra*. The influence of the *Rāmacaritā Mānas* of Tulsidas on Gandhi is next to that of the *Gītā*. He was also greatly influenced by the life and teachings of Swami Vivekananda. His conception of *Daridra Nārāyaṇa*, the poor as God, was adopted, elaborated and practised by Gandhi himself.

Dadabai Naoroji taught the first lesson of *ahiṃsā* to Gandhi, and Gokhale was the first Indian political leader who introduced the principles of religion into public life and tried to spiritualize it. Gandhi was much influenced by Gokhale whose politics appealed him. Gandhi inherited a lot from Dadabhai and Gokhale. He was also influenced by Sir Pheroz Shah and Lokmanya Tilak. Gandhi himself said:

> "Sir Pheroz Shah had seemed to me like the Himalaya, the Lokmanya like the ocean. But Gokhale was as the Ganges. One could have a refreshing bath in the holy river. The Himalaya was unshakable and one could not easily launch forth on the sea, but the Ganges invited one to its bosom."[111]

109 M.K. Gandhi, *My religion*, p. 9.

110 R.K. Prabhu and U.R. Rao (eds), *The mind of Mahatma Gandhi*, p. 94.

111 M.K. Gandhi, *An autobiography*, p. 133.

Western Influences

Gandhi was influenced by the Western thinkers, writers and prophets who are both ancient and modern. He owed indebtedness to the West. He did not think that everything Western had to be rejected. He learnt about *ahiṃsā* from the Western tradition also. Thus says Gandhi:

> "I have nothing to be ashamed of if my views on '*ahiṃsā*' (nonviolence) are the result of my Western education. I have never tabooed all western ideas nor am I prepared to an athematize everything that comes from the west are inherently evil. I have learnt much from the west and I should not be surprised to find that I had learnt something about *ahiṃsā* too from the west."[112]

The ancient Greek philosopher, Socrates, as seeker of truth, influenced Gandhi greatly. Commenting on Socrates and his stand for truth, Gandhi pointed out:

> "Socrates would not refrain from preaching what he knew to be truth to the Athenian youth and bravely suffered the punishment of death. He was in his case a *Satyāgrahi*."[113]

Gandhi regarded Socrates as a great *Satyāgrahi*. He had great admiration for Socrates and found in him a soul force which is capable of fighting against injustice. Socrates was courageous enough to prefer a cup of hemlock to give up his pursuit of truth and resisted superstitious beliefs of his people through non-violent means.

The Persian and Islamic Influences

In South Africa, Gandhi came into contact with many good Christians and Muslims. Seth Abdullah, was among one of his

---

112 M.K. Gandhi, *Hindu dharma*, p. 199.

113 Gandhi, *The science of Satyagraha* (The quotation is part of the book.).

Muslim friend whose knowledge of *Holy Quran* was thorough and extensive. Gandhi said:

> "Contact with him gave me a fair amount of practical knowledge of Islam. When we came closer to each other, we had long discussions on religious topics."[114]

He further writes:

> "A friend recommended Carlyle's Heroes and Hero-worship. I read the chapter on the Hero as a prophet and learnt of the prophet's (Muhammad's) greatness and bravery and austere living."[115]

He also studied Washington Irving's *Life of Muhammad and His Successors,* and said, "These books raised Muhammad in my estimation."[116] Gandhi also came across Zoroastrianism. He said, "I also read a book called, *"The Sayings of Zarathustra."*[117] But he did not write much about the influence of the Zoroastrian religion on him. He took great ideas from every religion and from every quarter—both East and the West.

He said:

"I have always honoured and reposed faith in elders and wise men."[118]

Perhaps no contemporary Indian thinker has taken so much from all that is great and good from all major religions of the world. His greatness lies in digesting those ideas and formulating his philosophy of life and action from Indian standpoint.

---

114 M.K. Gandhi, *An autobiography,* p 78.

115 M.K.Gandhi, *An autobiography,* p.

116 *Ibid.,* p. 119.

117 *Ibid.,* p. 119.

118 Gandhi, *All men are brothers,* p. 217.

New Testament

New Testament, especially The Sermon on the Mount, went straight into his heart. Gandhi compared The Sermon on the Mount with the *Gītā* and referred to what Jesus said in the *New Testament, Mathew* 5: 39-40:

> "But I say unto you. That ye resist not evil but whosoever shall smite thee on Thy right cheek, turn to him the other also. And if any man will thee at the law, and take away thy coat let him have thy cloak also."[119]

These verses delighted him beyond measure. He was reminded of Shamal Bhatt's "For a bowl of water gives a goodly meal."[120] His young mind tried to unify the teachings of the *Gītā, The Light of Asia,* and The Sermon on the Mount.[121] He found the spirit of renunciation present in Sermon on the Mount appealed to him greatly. Gandhi says, I have not been able to see any difference between the Sermon on the Mount and the *Bhagavad Gītā*. What the Sermon describes in a graphic manner, the *Bhagavad Gītā* reduces to a scientific formula. It may not be scientific in the accepted sense of the term, but it has argued out of the law of love—the law of abandon as I could call it in a scientific manner. The Sermon on the Mount gives the same law in wonderful language. *The New Testament* gave me comfort and boundless joy as it came after the repulsion that part of the old has given me. Today supposing I was deprived of the *Gītā* and forgot all its contexts but I had a copy of the Sermon, I should derive the same joy from it as I do from the *Gītā*.[122] Gandhi's Christian friends taught him the essence of Christianity.[123] According to Gandhi:

---

119 M.K. Gandhi, *The story of my experiments with ruth,* p. 51.

120 *Ibid.,* p. 51.

121 *Ibid.,* p. 102.

122 *Young India,* 22.12.1927, p. 426.

123 Louis Fischer, *The life of Mahatma Gandhi, Part.1,* p. 59.

> "Jesus was one of the greatest teachers that the humanity has ever produced. He held that Jesus does not belong solely to Christianity alone, but to the entire world and all races and people."[124]

He read the *Holy Bible* and was impressed by the Sermon on the Mount. He says:

> "My young mind tried to unify the teachings of the *Gītā*, the *Light of Asia* and the Sermon on the Mount. That renunciation was the highest from of religion appealed to me greatly."[125]

Gandhi had immeasurable love for Christ but he did not like some aspects of Christianity. It has been said that Gandhi "embraced Christ but rejected Christianity."[126]

He wondered at the non-violent character of Christ and called him "The Prince of *Satyāgraha*". In England, Gandhi renewed the study of the *Bible* and admitted that Jesus played a great role in his life. He chooses several words from the *Bible* and referred it many times in his talks. Theosophy believes in the equality of all religions and considers them as the branches of one religion. Gandhi considered Leo Tolstoy as one of his best teachers. Commenting on Tolstoy, Gandhi aptly puts:

> "There is no doubt that there is nothing new in what Tolstoy preaches. But his presentation of the old Truth is refreshingly forceful. His logic is unassailable. And, above all, he endeavors to practise." The study of Tolstoy's *The Gospels in Brief* made an indelible impression on Gandhi. And he "began to realize more and more the infinite possibilities of universal love."[127]

---

124 *The modern review, October* 1941, p. 407.

125 M.K. Gandhi, *Autobiography*, p. 51.

126 Louis Fischer, *Gandhi: His life and message for the world*, p. 131.

127 M.K. Gandhi, *The story of my experiments with truth*, p. 119.

If a person lives too much for himself instead of feeding others, he not only loses possibility of giving away the surplus, but also by eating too much he is deprived of the power to help others. Tolstoy says:

> "To be good and lead a good life means to give others more than one takes from them."[128]

Tolstoy derived the concept of bread labour enunciated by the Russian writer and peasant philosopher T.M. Bondreff who stated: "If a man works not neither shall he eat." For Tolstoy it was "a test of sincerity in recognizing equality of all men." This helped Tolstoy to be nearer to the majority of the labour class from whom he was fenced by a war.[129] Gandhi was very much attracted towards the concept of 'bread labour'.

Next to Tolstoy, it was the modern writer John Ruskin who profoundly influenced Gandhi. Mr. Polak came to see off Gandhi at the railway station on his journey from Johannesburg to Durban and left with him a book to read during his journey. It was Ruskin's *'Unto This Last'*. It became impossible for Gandhi to lay aside the book. When once he started reading, it gripped him. Gandhi determined to change his way of life in accordance with the ideals presented in the book. It brought about an instantaneous and practical transformation in his life. He translated this book later into Gujarati entitling it as *Sarvodaya* (the welfare of all). Gandhi discovered some of his deepest convictions reflected in this book of Ruskin. The teachings embodied in this book understood by Gandhi are as follows:

1. "That the good of the individual is contained in the good of all.
2. That a lawyer's work has the same value as the barber's in as much as all have the same right of earning their livelihood from their work.

---

128 Leo Tolstoy, *Essays and letters*, p. 70.

129 Pyarelal, Mahatma Gandhi, *The early phase*, Vol. I, p. 667.

3. That a life of labour, i.e. the life of the tiller of the soil and the handicraftsman is the life worth living.

Gandhi said:

"The first of these I knew. The second I had dimly realized. The third had never occurred to me. '*Unto This Last*' made it as clear as daylight for me that the second and the third dawn, ready to reduce these principles to practice."[130]

Ruskin's main object was to give an accurate and stable definition of wealth. His second object was to show that the acquisition of wealth was finally possible only under certain moral conditions or society with the belief in the existence for the practical purpose, the attainability of honest. He held that the old and destitute have to be rehabilitated for their comfort.

"A labourer," says John Ruskin, serves his country "with his spade, just as a man in the middle ranks of life serves it with sword, pen, or lancet. If the service be less, and therefore, the wages during health less, but not less honourable; and it ought to be quite as natural and straight forward a matter for a labourer to take his pension from his parish, because he has deserved well of his parish, as for a man in higher rank, to take his pension from his country, because he has deserved well of his country."[131]

Gandhi was also influenced by the American anarchist, Henry David Thoreau. He wrote the book on Civil Disobedience. When Gandhi was imprisoned due to *Satyāgraha* campaign in South Africa, he read Thoreau's book with great interest. Gandhi defined Civil Disobedience as 'Civil breach of its sanctions'. He held that this expression coined by Henry

130 M.K. Gandhi, *The story of my experiments with truth*, p. 221.

131 John Ruskin, *Unto this last*, p. 6.

Thoreau signifies his own resistance against the unmoral laws of a slave state. He has left a masterly treatise on the duty of Civil Disobedience.

Gandhi criticized certain aspects of Western civilization but admired certain good things in it. He says:

> "I have condemned Western Civilization in no measured terms. I still do so, but it does not mean that everything Western should be rejected. I have learnt a great deal from the West and I am grateful to it. I should think myself unfortunate if contact with and the literature of the West had no influence upon me."[132]

Modern India vows much to Gandhi. He was essentially a man of religion who was forced by historical circumstances to join in politics and lead to new renaissance and freedom. His religious ideas are liberal, catholic and thought-provoking. He wrote and spoke extensively on religious matters:

> "In his discussions on religion, Gandhi was concerned first with defending the individual's right to believe in his own faith as long as that faith does not come into conflict with or not contradicted by ascertainable facts; second, with bringing the religious questions."[133]

Gandhi feels religious pursuit and secular craving can go together. And he also feels all work for the society and the country is also work of the God.

Concept of God

Gandhi had immense faith in God and he accepted that there is liberty to others to deny his existence. Those who want to deny his existence are at liberty to do so. He allows us freedom, and his compassion, commands, obedience to his will. Some may dispute his existences. He said that he is one of the willing of wise men

132 Gandhi, *Hindu dharma*, p. 181.

133 K.R. Rao, *Gandhi and pragmatism*, p. 169.

who believe in him and never tired of bowing to him and singing his glory. He believed in God-head in the form of Rama and Kṛṣṇa. But he considered it has both personal and non-personal aspects.[134] He considered that God is indescribable. He is all things to all men. He is truth and love, source of light and life.

Gandhi tried to differentiate between religion and religious practices. As Prof. Kabir puts it:

> "Religion is the sense of reality which sums up all experiences and religion in this sense is one and the same for all. Religious practices, on the other hand, deal with broad aspects of such experience and here and there may be inconsistency or even opposition between one religion practices and another."[135]

Gandhi believed that all religious practices would finally lead to the same goal since all religious practices derive from religious experience which is common to all mankind. He also accepts the Christian concept that God is love. But he thinks it is more appropriate to say that God is Truth. He says: "I would say with those who say God is love, God is love. But deep down in me I used to say that though God may be love, God is Truth, above all. If it is possible for the human tongue to give the fullest description of God, I have come to the conclusion that, for myself, God is Truth."[136] Let us follow his reasoning in his own words. He says:

> "But two years ago I went to step further and said that Truth is God. You will see the fine distinction between the two statements, viz., that God is Truth and Truth is God. And I came to the conclusion after a continuous and relevant search after truth which began nearly fifty years ago."[137]

134 "I do not believe God to be a personal being in the sense that we are personal beings. I understand God to be universal law."

135 Prof. Humayun Kabir, *Gandhian philosophy*, p. 27.

136 *Young India*, December 31, 1931, pp. 427-428.

137 *Young India*, December, 1931, pp. 427-428.

He also considered that it is only God that can love the truth. He says that God alone knows absolute truth. Therefore, he often said, Truth is God. It follows that man, a finite being, cannot know the absolute truth. It is not possible for anyone to become repository of absolute truth:

> "Nobody in this world possesses absolute truth. This is God's attribute alone. Relative truth is all we know. Therefore, we can only follow the truth as we see it. Such pursuit of truth cannot lead anyone astray."[138]

He says the word love also can be used for God. But it has many meanings and the human love in the sense of passion could become a degrading also. He argues:

> "I found too that love in the sense of *ahiṃsā* had only a limited number of votaries in the world. But I never found a double meaning in connection with truth and not even atheists had demurred to the necessity or power of truth. But, in their passion for discovering truth, the atheists have not hesitated to deny the very existence of God from their own point of view, rightly, and it was because of this reasoning that I saw that, rather than say that God is Truth, I should say that Truth is God."[139]

Faith

For Gandhi, the belief in God and universal spirit is not the result of any logical process:

> "He sometimes referred to God as a personality. At other times he regarded Him as the source of an inner voice. In every crisis of life he depended more on this inner voice or intuition than on the ordinary normal ways of human thought and reactions."[140]

---

138 *Harijan*, June 2, 1946, p. 167.

139 *Young India*, December, 31, 1931, pp. 427-428.

140 Humyun Kabir, *Gandhian philosophy*, pp. 26-27.

Gandhi felt that faith is an essential ingredient of religious experience. Without faith religions cannot have their existence. He says:

> "It is the faith that steers us through stormy seas, faith that moves mountains and faith that jumps across the ocean. The faith is nothing but a living, wide awake consciousness of God within."[141]

He says the faith of the people has a base in the reasoned experience of people who lived a life purified by prayer and penance. "It cannot wither under the slightest stormy weather. It is like the unshakable Himalayas."[142] He says that when we want to prove something using reason as the source and method we must use the rationalist method only and we should not bring in faith to buttress our argument.[143] Though reason has its role in human experience, it has certain limitations. He says:

> "Rationalists are admirable beings; rationalism is a hideous monster when it claims for itself omnipotence."[144]

Faith is something like the sixth sense. It has the capacity to transcend reason but it need not contradict reasons. "Faith is a kind of sixth sense which works in cases which are without the purview of Reason."

Prayer and Worship

Gandhi had immense faith in the power of prayer. He believed that prayer can give tremendous power to those who pray. He also said that prayer will help him get adequate power to gain Swaraj.

---

141 *Young India*, September 24, 1925, p. 331.

142 *Harijan*, January 26, 1934, p. 8.

143 *Young India*, September, 26, 1929, p. 316.

144 *Young India*, October 14, 1926, p. 359.

Gandhi writes:

> "Prayer has saved my life. Without it I should have been a lunatic long ago. I have had my share of the bitterest public and private experiences. They threw me into temporary despair. If I was able to get rid of that despair, it was because of prayer."[145]
>
> Further he says, "Prayer is the only means of bringing about orderliness and peace and repose in our daily acts."[146]

Gandhi's views on idol worship are interesting. He says about idol worship:

> "One may question on logical ground whether prayer and belief in God would help solve any real problems of life; but the possibility of their psychological effect on individual accepting them cannot be questioned. I do not disbelieve in idol worship. An idol does not exit any feeling of veneration in me. But I think that idol-worship is a part of human nature. We hanker after symbolism. No Hindu considers images to be God. I do not consider idol–worship a sin."[147]
>
> "He supports idolatry in so far as it helps one realize God."[148]

Image worship has been the battle-cry for ages and people supporting it have been evenly matched against those who denounce it. *Sanātani* Hindu regards image worship as the core of Hindu religion. Religion reformers such as Raja Rammohun Roy, Keshab Chandra Sen, Devendranath Tagore and Dayananda Saraswati have denounced it in unmistakable

---

145 Pattabhi Sitaramayya, *Gandhi and Gandhism*, pp. 227-228.

146 Gandhi, *Truth is God*, p. 43.

147 *Harijan*, March 6, 1937, p. 26.

148 Gandhi, *The unseen power*, p. 99.

terms. Ramakrishna Paramahamsa and Swami Vivekananda believed both in idol-worship and also the worship of the Formless.

Religion and Ethics

According to Gandhi, the practical aspect of religion is ethics. He believed that there are certain universal ethical laws. He said:

> "The true laws of morality can be ascertained and systematized only where men are prepared to devote themselves to their investigation with the same disinterested seal as in the case of the positive sciences."[149]

He criticized customary morality and he said there was neither good nor bad in such life. He said: "The question of morality does not enter at all into many of our ordinary sections, since we are, for the most part, the mere creatures of conventions."[150] An action, done with immoral motive, ceases to be moral. He said: "No action can be called moral, unless it is promoted by moral intention. The end cannot justify the means."[151]

Gandhi opined that the aim of one's own life must be liberation. But he did not develop it as a theory. He rejects the philosophy of salvation, which means cessation of existence and aloofness from the world. For him the self does not loose it's individuality in the Absolute, but keeps its individuality and unique existence in all its conditions. The soul does not cease to exist nor become God Himself. The souls being parts of God cannot become God himself. Soul, according to Gandhi, has limited existence and cannot become the whole of reality. He writes:

---

149 Gandhi, *Ethical religion*, p. 46.

150 Gandhi, *Ethical religion*, p. 35.

151 *Ibid.*, pp. 41-42.

> "Man will ever remain imperfect, and it will always be his part to try to be perfect, so that perfection in love or no possession will remain an unaltered idea so long as we are alive, but towards which we must ceaselessly strive."[152]

Gandhi accepts the Buddhist conception of Thathāgata. Individual salvation is not possible so long the entire humanity does not attain it. Unless all the selves in bondage attain liberation, it is impossible for him to realize God. He said:

> "I do not believe that an individual may gain spirituality and those that surround him suffer. I believe in the essential unity of man and for that matter of all that lives. Therefore, I believe that if one man gains spirituality, the whole world gains with him, and if one man falls, the whole world falls to that extent."[153]

Religion and Society

Gandhi never attempted to work out a systematic philosophy. He was a man of action and he never took pains to work out all the implications of what he believed. "My life is my message," he used to say. This attitude is peculiar to Indian tradition, though some of the Indian philosophical systems are known for their rigour, the stress on practical aspects is found in many of the *Ṛṣis* of ancient India. Gandhi held the view that it is not possible to know the truth, wholly for human beings. He says:

> "It is not given to man to know the whole truth, his duty lies in living up to the truth as he sees it, and in doing so, to resort to the purest means, i.e., to non-violence."[154]

---

152 M.K.Gandhi, *The modern review*, 1935, p. 412.

153 *Young India*, March 9, 1932, p. 141.

154 *Harijan*, November 24, 1933.

Gandhi was essentially a practical man and he was always praying for simplicity and took pragmatic view of most of human problems. Many found inconsistencies in his thought and action. He never hesitated to deviate from something he said before if the situation demanded it:

> "It is interesting to remember that he called his autobiography *My Experiments with Truth*. In other words he allowed the real world to make its impact on him and he reacted to its demands with the whole of his personality."[155]

He accepts that differences arise between followers of one religion and the other. It is mainly due to complex nature of human personality and diversity of religious practices. He says that the unity becomes apparent when the complexity is discarded and the basic yearning of the human mind for identification with the real revealed in its purity. Simplicity was thus governing passion with him—simplicity in thought, action, and simplicity in religious belief. But the stress on simplicity by Gandhi led some of his followers to believe that he preached poverty and thus some of his followers could not differentiate between the two.

His distinctive contribution lies in the approach that the man must change and in it lies the social and political wellbeing. Many Indian reformers in the 19th century believed that by ushering in social reform the individual himself will change. Gandhi did not accept the view. Gandhi held that it was only when the individual changes the society can be changed. He was a great fighter for social reforms: but he believed that social reforms would become effective only when the individual reformed himself. His, concept of liberation is not that of an ascetic confined to his cave of *sādhana*, religion has a bearing on society. He says: "The bearing of this religion on social life is, or has to be, seen in one's daily social contact

155 *Harijan*, March, 20, 1913.

to be true to such religion one has to lose oneself in continuous and continuing service of all life."[156] He further says:

> "Realization of Truth is impossible without a complete merging of oneself in, and identification with, this limitless ocean of life. Hence, for him no happiness on earth beyond or apart from it. Social service here must be taken to include every department of life. In this scheme there is nothing low, nothing high. For, all is one, though we seem to be many."[157]

Religious Pluralism

Mahatma Gandhi believes in religious pluralism. Just as there are many races in the world there are many religions. Thereby we should not compare one with the other to find out that ours is superior than the other. There must be mutual tolerance and appreciation of the other's religion. It is possible to attain salvation by following one's own religion, because essentially all religions in essence are the same. He says: "In reality there are as many religions as there are individuals."[158] He also says: "Religions are different roads converging upon the same point." He says: "I came to the conclusion long ago, after prayerful search and study and discussion with as many peoples as I could meet, that all religions were true and also that all had some error in them, and that, 'Whilst I hold by my own, I should hold others as dear as Hinduism, from which it logically follows that we should hold all as dear as our nearest kith and kin and that we should make no distinction between them."[159] He further says:

---

156 S. Radhakrishnan and Muirhead (eds), *Contemporary Indian philosophy*, p. 21.

157 *Ibid*.

158 Gandhi, *Hind Swaraj or Indian Home Rules*, p. 50.

159 *Young India*, January 19, 1928, p. 22.

> "Belief in one God is the corner-stone of all religions. But I do not foresee a time when there would be only one religion on earth in practice. In theory, since there is one God, there can be only one religion. But in practice, no two persons I have known have had the same identical conception of God. Therefore, there will, perhaps, always be different religions answering to different temperaments and climatic conditions."[160]

He says that all religions contain truth and that they are all God given, and he says, if one takes the pain of going through all these scriptures they will necessarily find that all of them contain the same truth. But to understand them we must take their standpoint and view their sayings in that light. Gandhi says:

> "I believed that, only all of us could read the scriptures of the different faiths from the standpoints of the followers of those faiths, we should find that they were all one and were all helpful to one another."[161]

Gandhi also considers that this expression "Truth is God" describes his definition of religion.

> "Denial of God we have known, Denial of Truth we have not known. The most ignorant among mankind have some truth in them. We are all sparks of Truth."[162]

Gandhi's Views on World Religions

From Gandhi's autobiography and other sources which indicate the religious development of Gandhi we find that he took much from many religions. He was born a Hindu, but his Hinduism was his own. It had its roots firm in ancient

---

160 *Harijan,* February 2, 1934, p. 8.

161 *Harijan,* February 16, 1934, pp. 5-6.

162 S Radhakrishnan and Muirhead (eds.), *Contemporary Indian philosophy*, p. 21.

Hinduism but it grew and developed in the light of his contact with other religions, more especially Christianity. He sought to drink at the spring of all religions, and, therefore, he felt that he belonged to every religion. And yet, if he had to have a level, the level he preferred and which was his not only by right of birth but also intrinsically, was Hinduism, the religion of his forefathers.[163] There was a time in Gandhi's life in South Africa, when he was attracted by the teachings of Christianity; they had lasting impression on his mind. But deep down in him there was faith in Hinduism. He felt his salvation was possible only by following his own religion. He considered Hinduism to be broad and all inclusive. He felt Hinduism is relentless search after truth.

> "If I were asked to define the Hindu creed I should simply say: Search after truth through non-violent means. A man may not believe even in God and still he may call himself a Hindu. Hinduism is a relentless pursuit after truth and if today it has become morbid, inactive, irresponsive to growth it is because we are fatigued: and as soon as the fatigue is over, Hinduism will burst forth upon the world with a brilliance perhaps unknown before, of course, therefore, Hinduism is the most tolerant of all religions. Its creed is all-embracing."[164]

He was an orthodox Hindu in many aspects and he based his beliefs on the Hindu scriptures. He never found it wanting and he found no necessity to change his faith. Hinduism was his life-breath, the very marrow of his bones and he clung to it through all his tempestuous career as a child to its mother's arms. He considered Hinduism to be all inclusive and free from dogma. Whatever good that is there in all other religions, he said, is found in Hinduism.

---

163 Gandhi, *My religion* (ed) B. Kumareppa, p. 3.

164 *Young India,* April 24, 1924.

He says:

> "On examination I have found it to be the most tolerant of all religions known to me. Its freedom from dogma makes a forcible appeal to me in as much as it gives the votary the largest scope for self-expression."[165]

Hinduism (he includes both Buddhism and Jainism) has found the highest expression of non-violence, though it is found in all religions in some degree. Hinduism believes in the oneness not of merely all human life but in the oneness of all that lives.[166] He feels that Hinduism also would have perished if it had one prophet and one book as the source of its religion. It is not based on any one God and on any one scripture. He says:

> "Hinduism is like the Gaṅgā pure and unsullied at its source, but taking in its course the impurities in the way. Even like the Gaṅgā it is beneficent in its total effect."[167]

Gandhi feels that Hinduism is most catholic of all religions. It is not difficult to find considering Islam to be most democratic of all religions. They appear at some places to contradict each other, because they came into existence at several periods of history, serving the religious and social needs of the people. If we dogmatically follow their dictates we are at confusion because we cannot know what to follow when two different scriptures ordain us in a different way in a particular situation. Gandhi says:

> "Knowledge is limitless and so also the application of truth. Everyday we add to our knowledge of the power of *Ātman*, and we shall keep on doing so. New experiences will teach us new duties, but truth shall ever be the same."[168]

---

165 Gandhi, *Hindu dharma*, pp. 5-6.

166 Gandhi, *Hindu dharma*, pp. 5-6.

167 *Ibid.*, p. 19.

168 *Ibid.*, p. 20.

Gandhi says that there is no proselytisation in Hinduism. Because he feels that it is wrong for a religious denomination to think that it alone is a repository of truth. They must be made to know the truth by accepting their belief. He further says that Hinduism has done lots of good to the world. It made great strides in the discoveries in things of spirit.

> "Just as in the west they have made wonderful discoveries in things of material, similarly Hinduism has made still more marvelous discoveries in things of religion, of the spirit of the soul."[169]

Thus though praises Hinduism as a great religion, he never considered that other religions are not equally great, or their contribution to the realm of spirit is less. But he felt Hinduism has a special mission. The most ancient records and then look round you and you would be constrained to say. 'Yes; I see here ancient India still living.'[170] He praises certain values, which he considered made Hinduism a great religion. Some of them are the idea or man's identity with the 'dumb oration', freedom from proselytisation which is a source of conflict between one community and another, its stress on living than on preaching what consider to be true, he also considered that the theory of transmigration and the institution of *Varṇāśrama Dharma* are some of the important contributions of Hinduism to humanity and world civilization.[171]

Christianity

Gandhi was influenced by Christianity and he had great veneration for the personality of Jesus Christ. Passages in the Sermon on the Mount went straight to his heart and echoed something in him which he had learnt in childhood at school like the famous Gujarati verse:

---

169 *Young India*, November 24, 1927.

170 *Ibid.*

171 *Ibid.*

> "If a man gives you a drink or water and you give him drink in return that is nothing. Real beauty consists in doing good against evil."[172]

The idea underlying this verse had made a powerful impression upon him, which was further deepened by the *Bhagavad Gītā* and given a permanent form by Tolstoy's *The Kingdom of God is within You.*

Gandhi, on father-son concept of Christianity, says that, it is wrong to consider that God has only one son and that was Jesus Christ. He felt the essential divinity of man and considered that if God has sons all of us are his sons.

> "If God could have sons, all of us were his sons, If Jesus was like God, or God himself then all men were like God and could be God himself."[173]

This position of Gandhi is based on the metaphysical position accepted as Hindu. Many systems of Indian philosophy accept that every soul is potentially divine. The general Indian religious tradition accepts God as an ultimate reality. But it also says that each and every individual is a part of that reality. So Gandhi could not appreciate the concept that Jesus was the son of God, which was mainly a concept of Semitic religions. In popular Hinduism also there is the concept of *Avatāra* or descent of Godhead into the world to uphold righteousness. But this descent is as God in human form but not as the son of God.[174]

Jesus was a great teacher. The very fact that he could achieve so much within such a short period of three years of his ministry indicates the greatness of him. They may be controlled but cannot be changed. There is so much of myth and legend around Jesus. It is natural. It is the same case with all religions.

---

172 Anand T. Hingorani, *The message of Jesus Christ,* p.V.

173 Anand T. Hingorani, *The message of Jesus Christ,* pp. 11-12.

174 *Harijan,* April 17, 1937.

Gandhi considers that Jesus had great message for the mankind. But, it is distorted in the West. He feels that Western civilization, though professes Christianity, is not following its tenets in its proper perspective. Of course, this dichotomy of profession and practice is found in all religions. According to Gandhi, "The Gospel of Jesus needs no preaching. It is great and its fragrance can be smelt far and wide. As such there is no necessity of propaganda."[175]

One of the greatest tenets of Christianity is its Gospel of love. He says Buddhism also taught the same Gospel. The Gospel of love is an important stage in the development of human civilization. Though it is found in all religions, it was given to Christianity and Buddhism to stress on this important concept. Every living faith must have within itself the power of rejuvenation if it is to live. Both Christ and Buddha were not only prophets but social reformers also.

Gandhi considers them as true *Satyāgrahis*.

> "Buddha fearlessly carried the war into the enemy's camp and brought down on its knees an arrogant priesthood. Christ drove out the money changers from the temple of Jerusalem and drew down curses from Heaven upon the hypocrites and the Pharisees. Both were for intensely direct action. But even as Buddha and Christ chastised they showed unmistakable gentleness and love behind every act of theirs."[176]

Gandhi considered religion to be a personal matter. He felt that there is no necessity to force others to change their faith. If a person does not find peace through his own faith he may try to find it in another. But there is no necessity as such to force others to change their religion:

---

175 *Harijan*, September 28, 1935.

176 *Young India*, May, 12, 1920.

He asks:

> "Why should I change my religion because a doctor who professes Christianity as his religion has cured me of some disease or why should the doctor expect or suggest such a change whilst I am under his influence? Is not medical relief its own reward and satisfaction?"[177]

Gandhi considered that Jesus preached a new life. Only by following the wishes of the Lord one can attain liberation. It is no use chanting his name. It was being, who said;

> "Not everyone that faith into me, Lord, Lord, shall enter into the kingdom of Heaven, but he that doth the will of my father who is in Heaven."[178]

The Law of Jesus was the law of love. The death of Jesus signifies the Law of Love. "Jesus lived and died in vain if he did not teach us to regulate the whole of life by the eternal law of Love."[179] The same Gospel was preached by Buddha six hundred years ago in the East. But in the Western world it was Jesus who preached the Gospel of love. The law that was prevalent before was an eye for an eye, and a tooth for tooth. He changed it. His law was "to receive two blows when only one was given, and to go two miles when you were asked to go one."[180]

Europe, today, though Christian in religion, does not represent the true Christian traditions. "Europe is today only nominally Christian. It is really worshipping mammon." It is said in the *Bible* that "it is easier for a camel to pass through the eye of a needle than for rich man to enter the kingdom." While this is the teaching of Jesus Christ, the modern European nations, who are Christian by faith, crave after material possessions. Gandhi also says that the national anthem of England indicates

---

177 *Harijan*, June 12, 1937.

178 *Harijan*, January 7, 1939.

179 *Young India*, December 31, 1931.

180 *Young India*, September 8, 1920.

the satanic nature of the European civilization, though it claimed to be followers of Christianity. "If Jesus lived in our midst he cannot approve what the Christian organizations are doing," he says.[181]

Gandhi had high regard for Islam and its prophet. But he cannot accept all that is said in the *Quran* just as was unable to accept all that is said in the scriptures of Hinduism. He feels that he can practise all that is good in other religions but he has no right to criticize the bad in other religions:

> "I have now here said that I believe literally in every word of the *Quran*, or for the matter of that, of my scripture in the world. But it is no business of mine to criticize the scriptures of other faiths, or to point out their defects. It is and should be, however, my privilege to proclaim and practise the truths that there may be in them."[182]

Gandhi was humble enough to accept that he follows all that is good in other religions. The things which appear as improper may be, he feels, due to some misapprehension in ourselves, and we must try to understand them with the help of some exponents of that religion. Only by following this method we can appreciate other religions and find significance in these faiths:

> "It is only through such a reverential approach to faiths other than mine that I can realize the principle of equality of all religions."[183]

Gandhi said, his view was that if one is sincere, one can understand the good in all religions. But no one should try to criticize a religion, unless it is his own. Only a man who followed that particular faith can know its faults. The criticism of an alien religion may be due to our ignorance of that religion. Thus he says:

---

181 *Young India*, September 22, 1921.

182 Gandhi, *Hindu dharma*, p. 245.

183 *Ibid*.

> "My own experience of the non-Hindu critics of Hinduism brings home to me my limitations and teaches me to be wary of launching on a criticism of Islam or Christianity and their founders."[184]

Universal Religion

Gandhi feels that no one should change his religion unless he is totally dissatisfied with his religion. Even if one wants to change, it should be voluntary and not forced by an external agency. If nations and religious minorities have to live in peace, it is possible only by appreciation of other views and other's religions. International fellowship is possible not by discarding religion or by making all the people in the world conform to one religion. If all religions had some truth, they have some myths also. No religion is perfect and no scripture is perfect. Even if they were perfect, they are not so in the present form. As such there is no use gloating over the greatness of one's own religion. So what is wanted is not a universal religion encompassing the whole world with a particular prophet and fixed scripture and set dogmas. What we want is not one religion, but fellowship of religions, each following his own religion, yet appreciating others' religions.

Impediments to Fellowship

Gandhi says: "I would not only not try to convert, but would not even secretly pray that anyone should embrace my faith…. Hinduism with its message of *ahiṃsā* is to me the most glorious religion in the world, as my wife to me is the most beautiful woman in the world."[185] So there should be no question whether people who believe that their religion is superior should be allowed or not. For inter-religious fellowship, it is essential that one must believe in the greatness of all the religions:

184 Gandhi, *Hindu dharma*, p. 245.

185 Gandhi, *The message of Jesus Christ*, pp. 52-53.

> "If the people are not prepared to tolerate one another's religious belief, there can be no international fellowship."[186]

There is an element of imperfection in all religions, though they are true. Gandhi says that after studying all religions, "I came to the conclusion that all religions were right but everyone of them was imperfect, imperfect naturally and necessarily, because they were interpreted with our poor intellects, sometimes with our poor hearts, and more often misinterpreted."[187] Some scholars are of the opinion that a new world order, where there is peace, is possible only by giving religion its right place. Some feel resurgence of religion means disturbance of peace. We may find instances wherein religion worked as a cohesive force to unite people and we may also see instances where religious fanaticism gave rise to bloody wars. Gandhi's plea for tolerance of other faiths is not mainly due to the fear of consequences of such an ideological or religious conflict, but because of his inherent belief in the innate truth of all religions.[188]

So there cannot be one religion, but fellowship of religions. But fellowship is possible only on the basis of equality. If one religious community feels superior than the other, it is not possible. One may help the other remove its errors but one should not destroy others' religion and foist his on them. If there is to be fellowship between one religion and the other, it is possible only on the basis of equality and appreciation. Gandhi felt that there cannot be universal harmony among various faiths unless one is appreciative and not simply tolerant of the values of others. The aim of the fellowship (of faiths) should be to help a Hindu to become a better Hindu, a Muslim to become a better Muslim, and a Christian a better Christian.[189] "Whether

186 *Ibid.*, p. 53.

187 Gandhi, *The message of Jesus Christ*, pp. 16-17.

188 *Harijan*, April 20, 1934, p. 73.

189 M. K. Gandhi, *My religion*, p. 29.

you are going to accept the position of mutual tolerance or of equality of all religions, we must have innate respect for other religions as we have for our own. Many scholars of comparative religion also feel that there is scope for a better world order when there is religious pluralism. There are three ways to unite the world on religion, (1) the way of displacement, (2) synthesis, and (3) reconception. Professor Booking feels that there will be reconception in all major religions:

> "The reconception contemplated takes place within each religion; it involves no abandonment of any religion, no stepping out of it, but its enlargement and development. What is suggested is that a religion, as a result of such reconception, will be not less itself but more itself; it will, so to speak, come to its true self as it is more responsive to that reality with which it has to do."[190]

General Estimates

Gandhi's contribution to modern Indian religious thought is noteworthy. Traditional Indian religious thought is mainly concerning individual's liberation. But Gandhi felt that religion has a bigger dimension. As Prof. K.R. Rao points out, "But men are not only religious beings, but also social and political beings. Therefore, the religious, the social, the political and the moral act on and interact with each other and any consideration of religion should take into account the other aspects of the cultural complex; conversely, all other aspects of life, politics, ethics, etc. must be derived and be consistent with religion."[191] Gandhi himself puts it:

> "You cannot divide social, economic, political and purely religious work into watertight compartments. I do not know any religion apart from human activity."[192]

190 Robert Lawson Slater, *World religions and world community*, p. 213.

191 K. R. Rao, *Gandhi and pragmatism*, pp. 172-173.

192 R K Prabhu and V.R Rao, *The mind of Mahatma Gandhi*, p. 71.

Thus Gandhi felt a sincere love for Truth that will bring together all people of all religions and ideologies. Earnest pursuit of Truth without prejudices can bring universal peace devoid of strife and struggle. Bondurant aptly remarks:

> "Gandhi never claimed to know the truth in any absolute sense. And he repeatedly reminded others that man's viability to know the truth required that he maintain an unceasingly open approach to those who differ from him."[193]

This approach indicates Gandhi's open and tolerant attitude on the question of truth. He believes that true religion and true morality are inseparably bound up with each other. He would reject any religious doctrine that conflicts with morality. He is prepared to accept unreasonable religious sentiment if it is not immoral. He says:

> "As soon as we lose the moral basis, we cease to be religious. There is no such thing as religion overriding morality. Man for instance cannot be untruthful, cruel and incontinent and claim to have God in his side."[194]

Gandhi to some extent accepted the social, cultural and historical aspects of religion, some may say as there is one God there must be one religion. But Gandhi did not accept this view. He says:

> "I do not foresee a time when there would be only one religion on earth in practice.... Therefore, there will, perhaps, always be different religions answering to different temperaments and climatic conditions."[195]

---

193 Joan Bondurant, *The conquest of violence*, p. 16.

194 *Young India*, November 24, 1921.

195 Gandhi, *Truth is God*, p. 54.

Gandhi's philosophy is a summation of all that is great and good of the teachings of the prophets. Thus his aim is to spiritualize politics, individual and social life. Gandhi is a follower of Jesus Christ, Buddha and Mahavira. Prof. P.T. Raju observes:

> "We may call him at least a follower of Christ in the true spirit not merely in word but also in thought and action. But he is also a follower of Mahavira, the founder of Jainism, in his teaching of non-injury, or Buddha in his teaching of peace and compassion and uplift of the down-trodden, and of both Christ and Buddha in his teaching of active love, for between the teachings of Christ and Buddha, the difference is one of shade, but not of colour."[196]

Prof. K. S. Murty considers that Gandhi resembles St. Paul and St. Augustine in his ideas. He says:

> "Mahatma Gandhi is not a philosopher in the sense in which Aristotle or Spinoz is: nor is he a philosophical theologian like Sankara or Aquinas. The two men whom he resembles most are St. Paul and St. Augustine."[197]

Gandhi realized that there is truth in all religions. Professor Murty further remarks: "Gandhi is a prophetic spirit beckoning people to concern themselves absolutely with absolute ends. He was not concerned with immediate things, with preservation of society, the advancement of civilization and material progress. His teachings will always remain a beacon light luring humanity and a driving force haunting mankind to lift itself up from the sordid details of the present."[198]

196 P. T. Raju, *Structural depths of Indian philosophy*, p. 546.

197 K. Satchidananda Murty, *Indian philosophy since* 1498, p. 58.

198 K. Satchidananda Murty, *Indian philosophy since* 1498, p. 58.

5

Dr. S. Radhakrishnan

Dr. Sarvepalli Radhakrishnan was born on 5 September 1888, at a small place, Tiruttani, forty miles to the north-west of Madras, now Chennai. He was the second son of Sarvepalli Veeraswamiah and Sitamma in a family of five boys and two girls. His ancestors had moved there about 150 years ago from the Andhra fishing village of Sarvepalli about 200 miles further north. His parents were Telugu Smarta Brahmins. Smarta Brahmins were usually strict ritualists, strong on Sanskrit learning, and traditionally monistic in outlook.

Tiruttani was known as a pilgrim centre. Radhakrishnan was brought up in a strict devotional atmosphere with the worship of the popular god Śiva and his consort, the Śakti or "energies" of Śiva, as well as the family's chosen god Kṛṣṇa. Upon passing the entrance examination of Madras University, Radhakrishnan entered Madras Christian College in 1904. He received B.A and M.A. degrees from the University of Madras in 1907, and 1909, respectively. In 1917 he was appointed Professor of Philosophy in the University of Mysore. In 1921, he was appointed to the most important chair in Philosophy in India, King George V Chair of Mental and Moral Science in the University of Calcutta, now Kolkata. In 1926, he was invited to Oxford University to work as a visiting Professor.

Radhakrishnan started Indian Philosophical Congress in Calcutta with the eminent people of philosophy. He received first honorary doctorate from Andhra University, Waltair in 1927. He was Vice Chancellor of Andhra University from

1931-36. He became Vice Chancellor of Benaras Hindu University in 1939, and Indian Ambassador in U.S.S.R. in 1949. He was Vice-President from 1952-62 and finally to the highest chair that people could offer, the President of India from 1962-67. A large number of works have been published throughout his career. He had been awarded with many honours both in India and abroad in his lifetime. He expired on 17 April 1975 at his own house in Chennai. Joad describes Radhakrishnan's metaphysical stand point thus:

> "The unique function which Radhakrishnan fulfills today is that of a liaison officer. He seeks to build a bridge between the traditional wisdom of the East and the new knowledge and energy of the West."[199]

Radhakrishnan's basic position is a kind of synthesis of *Advaita Vedānta* and the philosophy of absolute idealism; like *Vedāntin*, he believes that the reality is one and like the absolute idealist he shows that everything is a necessary aspect of the one. B.K. Lal says that his philosophy may broadly be described as a philosophy of monistic idealism. He says:

> "It is monistic because reality is conceived as one, and it can be called idealism for reasons more than one. His idealism is of course metaphysical, but metaphysical idealism may be either idea-ism or ideal-ism. The former means that reality is of the nature of an idea—that it is mental or spiritual. Radhakrishnan also conceives reality as spiritual, and therefore he is an idealist. Ideal-ism, on the other hand, emphasizes the ultimacy and value of some ideal. Radhakrishnan prefers this sense of the word 'Idealism' and himself acknowledges that his philosophical point-of-view is an idealistic point-of-view in the sense that it believes that there is a spiritual ideal towards which the entire world-process is progressing."[200]

199 C.E.M. Joad, *Counter attacks from East*, p. 38.

200 B.K. Lal, *Contemporary Indian philosophy*, p. 259.

Because of this distinct tradition in the East, some of the original ideas of some thinkers are attributed not to their creative genius, but to a legendary king or *Ṛṣi*. Radhakrishnan followed this tradition and wrote more as an exponent of Indian philosophy than as an original thinker. He brought out new meanings from these old conceptions, which also need originality and depth of analysis and performance of this task is no way inferior to those displayed in founding a system.[201] Radhakrishnan considers that the development of one's own philosophical ideas is essentially based on one's own experience. He writes:

> "My thinking had, however, another source. It proceeded from my own experience, which can never be the same as the experience one acquired from reading or study. It is born of spiritual awareness rather than deduced from logically ascertained premises. Philosophy is produced more by our encounters with reality than by our historical study of those encounters."[202]

Self

The Self, according to Radhakrishnan, is an emerging structure. It is a unity which is more than some of its parts. The whole cannot be explained in terms of its parts. The Self is neither mere body nor it is simply consciousness. He says that the Self is a unity which is more than a sum of its subordinate parts. It is an active living whole, a body-mind, the latest term in the evolution process.

The concept of Self is neither static nor a self identical entity. Self is a mind-body organic whole, both consciousness and body continuously changes. The consciousness and the

201 Prof. Muirhead, wrote in his review of idealistic view of life, *Hibbert Journal*, October, 1932.

202 S. Radhakrishan, *The religion of spirit*, p.7.

body is in constant change. The parts of the Self also ceaselessly change. Therefore, Self is dynamic and changing reality. It is an emergent principle which comes into being, changes and passes away. Though the parts change constantly giving way to new parts, the whole is not destroyed with its parts. He says that Self has no element which is self identifiable throughout. The body is continuously changing….. there is nothing concrete in the individual which is not produced and which will not pass away, nothing from which there is no escape, or change, the distinctiveness of selfhood does not lie in its simplicity but in the specific organization of its contents.

There is difference between selves; all are not alike. The human self has a higher and internal unity than the animal self. The higher synthesis in the human self makes us capable of reflecting on experiences. According to Radhakrishnan, the Self undergoes change and in the series of changes in the Self, the unity is preserved in its attainment of end. The Self is an organization and it develops gradually, as the whole determines the function of the individual.

He thinks that there are two selves in man—the empirical and transcendental self. The empirical is the mind-body organism and the transcendental is a part of God.[203] Radhakrishnan believes that no *Jīva* can attain salvation unless and until all the *Jīvas* of the universe obtain their salvation. Some of the followers of Sankara hold this view. Similarly, Mahayana Buddhism maintains that it is impossible for a Jiva to attain salvation apart from the others. It exhorts, "All the enlightened ones not to enter *nirvāṇa* until they see that the rest of the creation too is enlightened." Though Radhakrishnan himself uses the word "Soul," he shows a definite preference of "Self" to express the ultimate spiritual reality and the participated spiritual reality in man.[204]

---

203 S. Radhakrishnan, *Indian philosophy*, Vol. II, pp. 538. 595, 596.

204 S. Radhakrishnan, *The Brahma Sutra*, p. 286.

God–Absolute

Radhakrishnan's theory of soul is corollary to his theory of God. The world cannot become one with the Absolute until the world and God become identical. God must continue to be God as long as the world lasts. Similarly, the *Jīva*, or the individual soul, which is created by God, also must remain with God, enters the Absolute only when there is no world and there will be no world only when there are no more *Jīvas* to be liberated. In the *Vedānta* system, the concept of Absolute and the concept of God are important and reconciliation of these two concepts is necessary. Radhakrishnan also tries the same. He says that the ordinary mind can picture the Absolute only in the form of God. The Absolute is a transcendental existence. But it is also capable of immanence. God is one of the infinite powers of the Absolute and it is also one of the projected powers of the Absolute.

According to Radhakrishnan, God and the Absolute are not exclusive concepts; they are unrelated. Both God and the Ultimate Reality are infinite and divine and exalted over all that is finite and the limited. He says that while the Absolute is the transcendent divine, God is the cosmic divine. He felt that the chief problem in the philosophy of religion has been the problem of finding a reconciliation of the concept of "Absolute with God". He considers that they are not mutually exclusive. He says that God, who is the creator, sustainer and judge of this world, is not totally unrelated to the Absolute. God is the Absolute from the human end. When we limit down the Absolute to its relation with the actual possibility, the Absolute appears as supreme wisdom, love and goodness. God is limited by selves and the cosmos. He helps the ignorant in spiritualizing them. He writes that if God has no environment on which He acts, He cannot be personal. If God is personal, He cannot be the Absolute which has nothing which is not included in it in every possible sense of the world. He writes:

> "God transcends the cosmic process with its whole contents of space and time. He transcends the order of nature and history until his being is fully manifested. When the moment arises, the world becomes flesh, the whole world is saved and the historical process terminates. Until then, God is partly in potential, partly in act. This view is not pantheistic, for the cosmic process is not a complete manifestation of the Absolute."[205]

Radhakrishnan considers the Ultimate Reality to be impersonal *Brahman*. This acceptance on the part of Radhakrishnan naturally leads him to the conclusion that theistic conception of God is to be transcended in the ultimate spiritual experience. He says:

> "While the character of God as personal meets certain religious needs, there are other needs that are not fulfilled by it. In the highest spiritual experience, we have the sense of rest and fulfillment of eternity and completeness. These needs have provoked from the beginning of human reflection, conceptions of the Absolute as pure and passionless being which transcends the restless turmoil of the cosmic life."[206]

He further says: "If God is bound up with the world subject to the category of time, if his work is limited by the freedom of man and the conditions of existence, however he may be in the quality of his life, in power, knowledge and righteousness, he but an expression of the Absolute."[207] Radhakrishnan's concept of the ultimate reality is idealistic and absolute and in idealism, as pointed earlier, it is nearer in many aspects to the absolute idealism of Sankara. He declares:

205 Muirhead and S. Radhakrishnan (ed). *Contemporary Indian philosophy*, p. 501.

206 S. Radhakrishnan, *An idealist view of life*, p. 349.

207 *Ibid.*, p. 343.

> "It is my opinion, that system plays the game of philosophy fairly and squarely, with freedom from pre-suppositions and with religious neutrality, and in Absolute idealism."[208]

The Absolute is pure. It is alone and unmanifest. It is nothing yet all things. It is beyond any form of expression and yet it is the basis of all expression. It is the one in whom all is found and yet all is lost. This is a typical description of the Absolute and Radhakrishnan subscribes to the definition of the Absolute. He describes Ultimate Reality as "Absolutely different, the beyond who cannot be comprehended by our concepts or recognized by our undertaking. He can only be described negatively or through seemingly contradictory descriptions."[209]

Religious Experience

Radhakrishnan has written extensively on all aspects of religion. He considers that religion is discipline of the soul which effects the transformation and integration and purification of the entire human personality. It is a means for the attainment of human integrity and is reached by a complete mastery over nature. Religion is not theological learning or dialectical skill. It has two sides, the individual and the social. Both sides are interdependent and complementary to each other and without the one the other is ineffect, it must lay emphasis on individual culture and purification and transformation of the inner world of man. Radhakrishnan considers that:

> "Religion is a means for the fostering of the integration of personality, of social equality and of respect for all living faiths."[210]

---

208 D.M. Datta, *S. Radhakrishnan and contemporary philosophy*, p. 671.

209 S. Radhakrishnan, *Eastern religion and Western thought*, p. 298.

210 S. Radhakrishnan, *Presidential speeches*, p. 234.

Radhakrishnan gives little importance to external aspects of religion. Religion is in man but not in his creeds. He said that true religion is in the heart of man, not in the man-made creeds. It believes in the spiritual nature of man, the essential divinity of the human soul. All religions emphasize this aspect. Like Gandhi, he feels that religion should inculcate moral values. If not, it is no religion. Religion must be ethical and at the same time based on rationality. He says:

> "Anything which makes us hate others is not religion. It is the opposite of religion. If religion is to be a binding force, it should become both rational and spiritual. It should encourage tolerance and understanding. Otherwise, it is not religion."[211]

Radhakrishnan said that no religion can be regarded as qualifying itself for being a true religion if it encourages such abnormal practices which are repugnant to the ethical sense of man. So no spiritual life can be true if it is not at the same time absolutely ethical.[212] On the function of Religion, he further remarks that the impact of religion should be found in every aspect of life and it should not stifle our rationality. He further said:

> "Religion must establish itself as a rational way of living. Religion must express itself in reasonable thought, fruitful action, and right social institutions."[213]

Yet, he feels that though religion influences our life in many facets. It is something more than that. He remarks: "I soon became convinced that religion is an autonomous form of experience which cannot be confused with anything else, not even with morality, though it cannot help expressing itself in a high code of morality. Religion is essentially a concern of the

211 *Ibid.*, p. 260.

212 S. Radhakrishnan, *Presidential speeches*, P. 26.

213 S. Radhakrishnan, *My search for truth*, p. 10.

inner life. Its end is to secure spiritual certainty which lifts life above meaningless existence or dull despair."[214] He says that: "Religion is not a creed or a code but an insight into Reality." It is dynamic and changes to suit the needs of the time. Religion must be creative and prepared to take new challenges.

> "So long as any religious system is capable of responding creatively to every fresh challenge, whether it comes by the way of outer events or of ideas, it is healthy and progressive. When it fails to do so it is on the decline."[215]

Intuition and Intellect

Radhakrishnan discusses extensively on the role or intuition and intellect in understanding the ultimate reality. Intuition should not be regarded as an alternative to reason; nor must it be regarded as a way of knowing which distinguishes mystical experience from philosophic endeavour. He says:

> "The *Vedāntins*, following Sankara, came to the conclusion that Spirit and *Brahman* were beyond the intellect and could only be directly experienced through intuition. But did not take the trouble to show clearly that this direct experience is a form of knowledge involved in and presupposed by the discursive knowledge of the intellect; and that the intellect is not necessarily opposed to this higher experience but is absorbed in it and completed by it."[216]

Intuition is a form of knowledge. It is different from mystical vision. For mystical awareness Radhakrishnan prefers to use then the 'integral experience'. He says:

---

214 *Ibid.*, p. 10.

215 S. Radhakrishnan, *Indian religion*, p. 5.

216 A. Schipp (ed.) *Philosophy of Sarvepalli Radhakrishnan*, p. 530.

> "It is unfortunate we are obliged to use the single term 'intuition' to represent scientific genius, poetic insight, ethical conscience as well as religious faith. Though these diverse movements represent the integrated activity of the mind, the activity is oriented towards knowing in some cases, enjoyment or creation in others."[217]

All varieties of cognitive experience result in a knowledge of the Real. It is produced in three ways. They are sense experience, discursive reasoning and intuitive apprehension. Through sense experience, we can know the outer characters of the external world. By means of it we obtain an acquaintance with the sensible qualities of the objects. Logical knowledge is obtained by the process of analysis and synthesis. Both sense knowledge and rational knowledge are the means by which we acquire control over our environment.

Intuition is direct knowledge and in it the distinction between the knower and the known is completely absent. It is knowing by becoming. Sense experience can explore only the external aspect of an object, whereas intuition can know the essence and it does not need verification. Verification is needed only when ideas are related to objects and when there is a difference between 'knowing a thing' and 'being a thing'. Intellectual knowledge is different from intuitive knowledge. Intellectual knowledge is not free from doubt when equally powerful argument is there to oppose it. But we need intellect for the expression and justification of the results of intuitive knowledge.

Religion and Ethics

Discussing about ethics, Radhakrishnan remarks: Right conduct is whatever expresses our real unity with God, man, and nature: wrong conduct is whatever does not bring out

217 S. Radhakrishnan, *An idealist view of life*, p. 200.

this essential structure of reality. The unity of the universe is the basic principle. Good is whatever advances towards completeness, and evil is whatever is in consistent with it.[218] Man, of course, needs an ethical ideal, but he cannot live on its abstraction alone. He said that man's needs as man and as a spiritual, transcending being must be taken into account.[219] He further said that it is because our ethical Self realizes only in part it aims whereas the transcending self in us reaches realization in its totality and fullness,[220] there is connection between the ethical and the transcendental, as a means to an end, and as a dynamic movement to that end.[221] Radhakrishnan made critical analysis of the ethics of the *Upaniṣads* and the *Bhagavad Gītā*. He says that moral action, according to *Upaniṣads*, is grounded in its basic aim to become one with the Absolute. The concept of morality, both internal and external, is subordinated to the one and only ideal. This ideal is an end in itself and morality is a means to that end. "Whatever ethics we have in the *Upaniṣads* is subsidiary to this goal."[222] Radhakrishnan uses the concept of *dharma* as the first principle in his ethical system. It is a principle because it is at one and the same time the origin and source of morality and it is the first principle and it cannot be reduced to another principle.

The *dharma* is eternal and it governs cosmic and human existence. It can be considered as equivalent to natural law. According to Radhakrishnan, every being through its natural constitution has its *dharma* or function. The concept of *dharma* is one of the ancient concepts and it has its roots in the *Vedic* concept of *ṛta* which stands for the cosmic and moral order and expresses the reasonableness and law abidingness of nature. It

218 S. Radhakrishnan, *The theism of the Bhagavad Gita*, p. 70.

219 S. Radhakrishnan, *Indian philosophy, Vol. I*, pp. 275-76.

220 S. Radhakrishnan, *An idealist view of life*, pp. 273, 305.

221 S. Radhakrishnan, *Eastern religions and Western thought*, p. 63.

222 S. Radhakrishnan, *Indian philosophy*, p. 208.

includes law and convention, etiquette and moral principles. There is continuity from the *Vedic ṛta* to the *Upaniṣad* and later *dharma*, and this continuity is facilitated by the notion of *Satya*.[223]

He further said:

> "*Dharma* maintains the cosmic order and moral harmony. Everything on earth will pass away but *dharma* will last forever and hence the imperative necessity of the practice of *dharma*."[224]

Dharma gives coherence and direction to the different activities of life. It is not a religious creed or cult imposing on ethical or social rule. It is the complete rule of life, the harmony of the whole man who finds a right and just law of the living.[225] The aim of *dharma* is to take the natural life of man and subject it to control without unduly interfering with its largeness, freedom and variety. Elaborating the concept of *dharma*, he says:

> "The *dharma* is a code of conduct supported by the general conscience of the people .... It is the system of conduct which the general opinion, or the spirit of the people supports, what the Germans call 'Sittlichkeit'. The *dharma* does not force men into virtue, but trains them for it. It is not a fixed code of mechanical rules, but a living spirit which grows and moves in response to the development of the society."[226]

The term *dharma* is one of complex significance. It stands for all those ideals and purposes, influences and institutions that shape the character of man both as an individual and as a member of society. It is the law of right living, the observance

---

223 A. Cichael, *Hindu moral life and action*, p. 130.

224 S. Radhkrishnan, *Brahma sutra*, p. 158.

225 Hughes (ed), *The individual in East and West*, p. 115.

226 S. Radhakrishnan, *Indian religions*, p. 61.

of which secures the double object of happiness on earth and salvation; it is ethics and religion combined. The life of a Hindu is regulated in a very detailed manner by the laws of *dharma*. His fasts and feasts, his social and family ties, his personal habits and tests are all conditioned by it.[227] Radhakrishnan considers that the ideal of ethics is self-realization. Moral conduct is self realized conduct. Self is not the empirical self, with all its weakness and vulgarity, selfishness and smallness, but the deeper nature of man. Free from all fetters of selfish individuality.

Religion and Society

Radhakrishnan believes in the efficacy of religion as a force which can transform the society and which, according to him, is a great cementing force between one community and another, between one nation and another. In his Kamala lectures he took up the issue of social reconstruction in the light of religious ideals. He considers the reconstruction of society on the basis of religious ideals only can save the humanity from impending dangers and considers that many of our present-day problems are due to our disinterest in the things of the spirit.

In this process of evolution of a better world order, there are bound to be convulsions in the form of revolutions and wars. They are growing pains of the society, before it reaches a new equilibrium. Even though there may be setbacks and relapses, the human race is bound to move towards the same world. Our efforts will transform society and build a new world order. It needs a lot of suffering on our part and we may have to make tremendous sacrifices for ushering in such a society. Radhakrishnan thinks that the energy necessary for social reconstruction comes form the religion. He says:

227 S. Radhakrishnan, *Indian religions*, p. 71.

> "Religion tells us that the creative energy necessary for drastic reconstruction comes from communion with the eternal. Fellowship and service spring from spiritual sources."[228]

Religion is for profound dissatisfaction with the existing state of humanity and an active preparation for a new life. Religion demands the most radical transformation of man and society. It will not be content until a new social order with basic economic justice, racial brotherhood and equality, free intellectual and spiritual cooperation and true friendship among the nations is established. The truly religious people are those who fight against injustice. Religion has a great role to play in the promotion of art and culture. Radhakrishnan points out the positive and negative aspects of religion. He aptly puts:

> "In spite of the great contributions of religions, through the ages, have made for the promotion of art, culture and spiritual life, they have been vitiated by dogmatism and fanaticism, by cruelty and intolerance and by the intellectual dishonesty of their adherents. So long as religions adopt their principles to the ruling interests of this world, so long as they support the established order however iniquitous it may be, those who revolt against such practices are the truly religious people."[229]

Religion should lead to fellowship. It has a civilizing function. He remarks: religion may start with the individual but it must end in a fellowship… the religious soul returned from the contemplation of Ultimate Reality to the care of practical life. This fact is illustrated in the lives of the great teachers like Buddha and Sankara who shared in the social and civilizing function of religion.[230] Religion has a role to play in society. In building human society religion has equal importance as that

228 S. Radhakrishnan, *East and West in religion*, p. 124.

229 Radhakrishnan, *East and West in religion*, p. 32.

230 Radhakrishnan and Muirhead, *Contemporary Indian philosophy*, p. 475.

of science. Radhakrishnan observed the work of rebuilding human household, the role of religion is no less important than that of science. The human individual consists of body, mind and spirit. Each requires its proper nutriment. The body is kept trim by food and exercise, the mind is informed by science and criticism, and the spirit is illuminated by art and literature, philosophy and religion.[231]

Science and Religion

The science and religion, according to Radhakrishnan, are not opposed to each other. He says: "The general impression that the spirit of science is opposed to that of religion is unfortunate and untrue." The spirit of science does not suggest that the ultimate beginning is matter. "We may split the atom. The atom of man which splits it is superior to the atoms. The achievements of science stand as witness to the spirit in man. The nature of the cosmic evolution with its order and progress, suggests the reality of underlying spirit."[232] It is wrong to imagine that science and technology are indifferent to the values of spirit.

> "The great advance of science reveals not the omnipotence of matter, but the superiority of the human mind to the world of matter. Sciences reveal to us the mastery at the heart of the universe. They disclose to us the riches of the spiritual life."[233]

But religion must serve the needs of the society and satisfy the scientific temper. He said that no religion can hope to survive if it does not satisfy the scientific temper of our age, sympathies with its social aspirations and foster the unity of the world.[234] Radhakrishnan observes that it is wrong to think that science and religion are opposed to each other. Science and religion represent

231 Radhakrishnan, *East and West in religion*, p. 45.

232 S. Radhakrishnan, *Indian religions*, p. 6.

233 S. Radhakrishnan, *The spirit of religion*, p. 23.

234 S. Radhakrishnan, *The spirit of religion*, p. 29.

two domestications to the human being, the rational and the spiritual. These two things cannot be divorced from each other; they must be coordinated, they must be integrated, they must be correlated, if a human being is to become really a human being. We need true religious sense and wisdom for using these great instruments for the purpose of human welfare. Development of science to some extent, weakened the religious spirit. He says:

> "The increase of knowledge and progress of material conditions have lead to a weakening of interest in the life of the spirit. The scientific temper which has become a part of modern man's mental equipment finds it difficult to accept religious beliefs and dogmas. They seem to obstruct the path to natural truth and moral progress."[235]

But there are certain final limits which scientific knowledge cannot overcome. There are gaps between the inorganic and the organic, between life and mind, and between mind and spirit that we cannot bridge. Progress of scientific knowledge discloses the existence of limits to it. However, Radhakrishnan is highly appreciative of the spirit of science and its achievements. He said that the spirit of science which has resulted in such great advances from steam to electricity, from electricity to atomic power, from atomic power to space travel, has brought the world together and made it a world in which nations and cultures are brought into close intimacy.[236] He also says that science is nearer to philosophy and religion.

> "The essential aim of all scientific disciplines is the knowledge of reality, that you should have a personal insight into reality. That is the purpose of science. It is wrong, therefore, to think that science leads us one way and religion leads us another."[237]

---

235 S. Radhakrishnan, *The fellowship of the spirit*, p. 4.

236 S. Radhakrishnan, *Presidential speeches*, p. 30.

237 *Ibid.*, p. 80.

Science is part of the attempt to understand the world and is not divided from philosophy and religion. They are all concerned with fundamental problems and concepts. Even science does not say now that the intangible is not existent. There is affinity between science and religion which is not dogmatic. General science is tentative in statement and provisional in conclusion, whereas religion has been certain and absolute. But science is not hostile to the spirit of religion but to its dogmas, but all religions are not dogmatic and there are degrees and level of dogmatism.

Christianity

Radhakrishnan is highly appreciative of Christianity's role in shaping the civilization. He says Christianity did not arise in a vacuum. It had obvious relations with the *Old Testament*, and other currents in Judaism. It is a dynamic religion prepared to adjust and modify to the changing needs. The main contributions of Christianity, in Radhakrishnan's opinion, are its emphasis on the insufficiency of the intellectual and the importance of the historical. Revelation is common to both Judaism and Christianity. Thirdly, both Judaism and Christianity believe not in the Greek view of God as unmoved mover, but in the living God. Judaism and Christianity accept God as a supreme person who reveals his will, who is a law-giver, who rules both the physical and the moral worlds and another characteristic of Christianity in addition to those that it derives from Judaism is that it believes in the doctrine of Incarnation.[238]

According to Radhakrishnan, there are certain drawbacks in the Christian tradition. He held that its emphasis on the doctrine of Incarnation is incompatible with its faith in the absolute and non-historical character of Godhood. He also points out that it is not reasonable to hold that righteousness is the will of God. Anything is right or good not because God's will permit it but because it is right and good. Secondly, such

238 H.N. Singh, *Contribution of S. Radhakrishnan to Indian religious thought*, pp.99-100.

a view bangs the door against all changes and progress. The other defect that Radhakrishnan notices in the tradition is that they invented the myth that only one religion could be true. Radhakrishnan feels some tenets of Christianity are Eastern and some Western. He remarks:

> "The characterization of intuitive realization, non-dogmatic toleration, as well as insistence on the non-aggressive virtue and universalist ethics, marks Jesus out as a typical Eastern seer. On the other hand, the emphasis on definite creeds and absolutist dogmatism, with its consequences of intolerance, exclusiveness and confusion of piety with patriotism, are the striking features of Western Christianity."[239]

Christianity is a syncretistic faith, a blend of various earlier creeds and remarks that it has ceased to be a religion of growth and freedom and became one of regimentation. To consider that Church is the bearer of revelation is authoritative in character. Radhakrishnan is against the dogmatism of the Church but he also says that "Jesus' religion was one of love and sympathy, tolerance and inwardness."[240] About Islam he says that it is a religion without mastery.

> "Its simplicity is its strength and beauty. It does not indulge in any theological subtleties, supernatural paradoxes or metaphysical pretensions. It is natural religion with one central principle that God makes, upholds, governs and perfects all things. This serene lofty theism is best suited for the simple-minded and unsophisticated. On its institutional side, it is perfectly rational. It has no castes or priests, requires no sacrifice or ceremonial, recognizes no ritual likely to distract the mind from the thought of the one God."[241]

239 S. Radhakrishnan, *East and West in religion*, p. 58.

240 S. Radhakrishnan, *Indian religions*, p. 123.

241 S. Radhakrishnan, *Indian religions*, p. 123.

Islam is opposed to materialism and believes that it leads to the downfall of man and nations. And it has no prejudice against any race, or colour and it is democratic in its structure. He says:

"Democracy is the key note of Islam on its practical side. That is what enabled it to succeed as a missionary religion. It involves every human being to its ample fold, whatever is his colour or race. It recognizes the capacity of all to become the servants of God."[242]

Religious Tolerance

Religious conflict is due to emphasis on one aspect of religion. Deeper analysis of religion leads us to the finding of a traditional unity of all religions. Religious conflicts do not touch the essence of religion. A person brought up in a particular religious tradition uses the symbols of that tradition and comes into conflict with another using other groups of symbols. Radhakrishnan says, "Religion is not a creed or a code but an insight into reality."[243] Man is always confronted with something greater than himself and religion is that discipline which makes man to "make a change in his own nature to let the Divine in him manifest himself."[244] Radhakrishnan has not hesitated to praise certain aspects of Marxism, a blatantly materialistic philosophy diametrically opposed to his own views. A.N. Marlow rightly points out:

> "So great is Radhakrishnan's imaginative sympathy with the views of others that he reminds us of Vachaspati Misra who commented on almost all the systems of Hindu thought, writing on each as if he believed in its doctrines."[245]

---

242 *Ibid.*, p. 123.

243 S. Radhakrishnan, *My search for truth*, p. 27.

244 *Ibid.*

245 A.N. Marlow, *Spiritual religion and the philosophy of Radhakrishnan*, p. 233.

According to Radhakrishnan, communism has all the characteristics of a religion though it is entirely secular and humanist. "It teaches us absolutely true a clear-cut philosophy of man and nature."[246] He says that every true religion has a note of revolutionary challenge. This note has disappeared in established religions, which have become purely formal. Communism has captured this note. As a matter of fact, he observes that there is hardly any phase in the history of community that has not its parallel in the history of Christianity.

Radhakrishnan feels that its methods and discipline remind one forcibly of certain religious order. It believes with religion that the world is on the brink of an apocalyptic cataclysm, an impending doom, that history is intolerably slow, that truth and justice must be established on Earth without delay, doubt or compromise. Communism is belief without God; it is the religion of atheism and it developed because religious people betrayed their responsibility and it is (communism) a judgement on the defects of religious practice. Radhakrishnan supports the view that every human being, every group and every nation has individuality worthy of reverence.

This view requires that we should allow absolute freedom to every religious group to cultivate what is most distinctive and characteristic of it. He says: "All peculiarity is unique and incommunicable, and it will be to disregard the nature of reality to assume that what is useful to one will be useful to everyone else to the same extent. The world is wide enough to hold men whose natures are different."[247]

As there are men at various stages of cultural developments, there are people at various levels of religious beliefs. Superstitious men and sub-cultures are found even in those religions which are generally considered to be advanced.

---

246 S. Radhakrishnan, *Recovery of faith*, p. 54.

247 S. Radhakrishnan, *The Hindu view of life*, p. 52.

This is found in Hinduism, Christianity and other religions.[248] Radhakrishnan feels that the spirit of tolerance must become universal as every nation and every religion are confronting the other nation and religion because of the rapid development of communication and transport systems. Those technological and other changes to some extent are changing the attitude of some religions which are supposed to be dogmatic.

The political ideal of the world is not so much a single empire with a homogeneous civilization, but a brotherhood of free nations differing profoundly in life and mind. He says that he sees no hope for the religious future of the world, if this spirit is not extended to the religious sphere also.

He says:

> "When two or three different systems claim that they contain the revelation of the very core and centre of truth and the acceptance of it is the exclusive pathway to heaven, conflicts are inevitable."[249]

He rightly remarked that belief is a unity which secures simple liberty not only for every type of organized life which has proved itself effective. The spirit of democracy with its immense faith in the freedom to choose one's ends and direct one's course in the effort to realize them makes for it nothing is good which is not self-chosen; no determination is valuable which is not self-determination.

Comparative Religion

Radhakrishnan hopes that there will be greater appreciation and understanding of the other man's religion. Of course, secularization and modernization are making the present-day man tolerant of the other man's faith, he believes that truth is in all religions. But because his concern for the religions

248 James Frazer, *Golden bough* (Abridged ed.) p. 56.

249 S. Radhakrishnan, *The Hindu view of life*, p. 58.

either of his own or the other is lessening. In the academic circles and in the serious students of religion, the comparative studies of religion to a great extent are opening up new vistas of inter-religious understanding. Radhakrishnan realized the importance of comparative religion.

He says:

> "When properly studied comparative religion increases our confidence in the university of God and our respect for the human race. It induces in us not an attitude of mere tolerance which implies conscious superiority, not patronizing pity, not condescending charity, but genuine respect and appreciation."[250]

Secularism

The concept of secularism is giving ground in all modern societies and the modern states take it as their policy. Radhakrishnan clears certain misconceptions about secularism. What is called as secularism is sometimes mistaken for neglect of religion or indifference to religion. It means this: "The aim of religion is the realization of the supreme and every pathway to it has to be recognized, validated and appreciated. That is the meaning of secularism. It does not mean that we do not care for religion. It means that we care for religion so intensely that we believe that everyone who is seeking the Divine, whatsoever pathway he adopts, is to be extended same kind of appreciation and encouragement to go forward."[251]

Different religions are not incompatible but complementaries. Every religion from the crudest to the modern has a function to play in shaping the life and conduct of its people. Further the stress on mystical aspect of religious experience than on authority or dogma also to a great extent widening the horizons of religious harmony.

---

250 S. Radhakrishnan, *East and West in religion*, p. 32.

251 S. Radhakrishnan, *Presidential speeches*, p. 342.

Dean Inge has pointed out that the centre of gravity in religion has shifted from authority to experience ..... The fundamental principles of mystical religion are now very widely accepted, and are, especially with educated people, avowedly the main rounds of belief."[252] Religious conflict is mainly due to shortsightedness of the religious leaders and institutionalization of the doctrines. Though religion is not for conflict, early church is. Radhakrishnan remarks:

> "Consider the repressive legislation of the Theodosius which by heavy penalties forbade the practice of any other religion than Christianity, the closing of the schools of philosophy at Athens by Justinian, the Albeigensim Crusades, the Dominican inquisitions, the Acts of supremacy and Uniformity in Elizabethan England, the religious wars of the Seventeenth Century and the cruelties perpetuated upon the Unbaptists."[253]

According to Radhakrishnan, the absolute truth goes beyond all forms and creeds, all historic revelations and institutions. He also observes that certain states considered Jesus as their own God and any attack on their country was an attack on God. St. Joan and the attitude of Anglican Church and Greek Church in Czarist Russia are some examples. So if one considers one's own religion is the only true religion, it is dogmatism. It is equally wrong to nationalize God for a nation's own self interest. Many attempts are made by some religions to bring the world's populace under one God and one Church forgetting the fact that the world can never be and should not be monolingual and mono-religious.

Radhakrishnan aptly points out:

252 S. Radhakrishnan, *The Hindu view of life*, p. 60.

253 S. Radhakrishnan, *East and West in religion*, pp. 64-65.

> "Nature has made many races with different languages, religions and social traditions and has set man to the task of creating order in the human world and discovering a way of life by which different groups can live peacefully together without resorting to force to settle their differences."[254]

He further says that the world is not intended to be a battle-ground of warring nations, but a common wealth of different groups cooperating in a constructive effort to achieve dignity, noble living and prosperity for all. Radhakrishnan's catholicity of approach represents the true spirit of ancient Indian tradition. As pointed by Radhakrishnan, it is not in the nature of things to have a monotonous unity and monolithic social structure and a universal religion. The history of the human race reveals that every attempt at universal religion and a universal state under one ideology has failed miserably. Radhakrishnan is critical of major religions of the world.

> "It is one of the major tragedies of the world that the great religions instead of uniting mankind in mutual understanding and goodwill divide mankind by their dogmatic claims and prejudices."[255]

The world has become a close neighbourhood. The distance between nations has reduced. Geographic distances are reduced by modern transport and communication system. The impact of man of the machines has shattered the pre-machine world of entirely independent states. We are heading towards a world society with a world economy. But this does not mean that it will lead to cessation of religious pluralism and ideological diversity.

---

254 S. Radhakrishnan, *Religion and society*, p. 13.

255 S. Radhakrishnan, *Fellowship of the spirit*, p. 5.

The history of world religions gives us a glimpse of the fact that religion has done immense good in organizing the semi-civilized societies, giving a purpose and meaning to their life and shaped their morality, ethics and orderly existence. Man's religion must be his own. It should not be imposed by anybody. Authoritarian religion may help one to some extent but it will not take one to the destination. He says:

> "A man's religion must be his own and not simply accepted on trust or imposed by authority. While trust and authority may put him on the way, it is his own independent search that will take him to the goal."[256]

Knowledge of other religions is necessary for religious tolerance. "If a man is to achieve wholeness for himself and for the world, if he seeks harmonious living he must know other religions."[257] The different religions should be regarded as comrades in a joint enterprise in facing the common problems of peaceful coexistence of the peoples, international welfare and justice, racial equality and political independence of all peoples. He believed that cooperation, not conflict, love, not hate, reason, not force, should govern human affairs and considers world civilization can grow on the basis of cooperation among religions.

> "All nations, small or large, have to work for peace, if they are to survive, and in the effort to preserve peace and freedom for all nations, we require, more than anything else, those moral and spiritual values of tolerance and understanding, of respect for the individual ideas, in which we share in common. We can work together and attain world fellowship on their basis."[258]

---

256 S. Radhakrishnan and Muirhead, *Contemporary Indian philosophy*, p. 503.

257 S. Radhakrishnan, *Fellowship of the spirit*, p. 39.

258 S. Radhakrishnan, *President Radhakrishnan's speeches and writings.*

India has produced Radhakrishnan, an academic philosopher, whose stature is not less than that of any other contemporary philosopher of Europe or America. J.H. Muirhead thought Bergson and Radhakrishnan occupy similar positions as leaders of thought in Europe and India.[259] Muirhead pointed out that Radhakrishnan's originality consisted in the depth with which he grasped the significance of what he said and made it dominate over details. Mackengie and McTaggart, Alexander and Russell considered that his contribution to absolute idealism has been substantial and important. G.P. Conger says:

> "Less ponderous than Royce, less meticulous than Bradley, less involved than Hegel, he (Radhakrishnan) has made idealism flow from a deep spring. By comparison, Eucken is provincial and Keyserling is trivial. Not since Fichte and Schelling has there been such a precipitate stream of inspiration."[260]

E.S. Brightman considers him as one of the greatest philosophers of mysticism in modern times.[261] Radhakrishnan did not adopt any particular religious tradition, but only recognizes that for philosophy religious experience is also important. He does not accept the whole of any religious tradition as superior to the evidence of the sense, but only that much of it which is logically coherent. No belief must be held merely because a scripture or a church sanctions it. Scriptural statements can never be superior to sense evidence and rational conclusions. Philosophy is entitled to and ought to take as its material not only empirical facts, the results of logical investigations and scientific knowledge, but also the spiritual intuitions contained in the scriptures and the writings of mystics and sages.

---

259 *Hibbert journal*, October, 1932.

260 P.A. Schlipp (ed.), *The philosophy* of *Radhakrishnan*, p.86.

261 *Ibid.*, p. 414.

There are different conceptions regarding Radhakrishnan's philosophy. P.T. Raju calls him as a follower of Sankara. Lawrence Hyde thought his attitude to the supreme was 'nearest of all' to that of Ramanuja and closely allied to that of Aurobindo. T.R.V. Murthy found that his philosophy stemmed as much from that of Sankara as from that of Nagarjuna.[262] But Radhakrishnan himself denied that he was the follower of any. Of course, he was greatly stimulated by what he studied. He commended in his writings the general spirit of Sankara's philosophy. But claimed that he thought on independent lines and developed a philosophy based on 'logical reflection, which is at once rational and spiritual. Prof. K. Satchidananda Murty says:

> "In his writings, ideas already known have come alive, acquired a new significance and gained relevancy to the present; connections between them have been shown and new ways of looking at the world and human existence and destiny, implicit in them, have been opened up. He has lifted up the beacon light higher; he has appealed to his generation and he has inspired many."[263]

Radhakrishnan also felt the Hindu religion was essentially other than that which was portrayed in the criticism of his teachers. Thus Radhakrishnan is both a critique of Hindu religion and defense of Hindu religion. Regarding the defense, he was inspired by the writings of Swami Vivekananda. He says:

> "The kind of thrill which we enjoyed, the kind of mesmeric touch that those writings gave us, the kind of reliance on our own culture that was being criticized all around—it is that kind of transformation which his writings effected in the young men in the early years of this century."[264]

---

262 P. A. Schlipp. *The philosophy of Radhakrishnan*, pp. 519, 378, 605.

263 K. Satchidananda Murty, *Indian philosophy since 1498*, p. 126.

264 S. Radhakrishnan, *Our heritage*, p. 97.

In this writing he affirmed *Vedānta* as the essence of Hinduism and in fact the essence of all religions. It was not a 'religion' but 'religion itself' and it is the religion of the spirit. By promoting this 'religion of the spirit' by defense, definition and promulgation of *Vedānta,* he believed he was participating as best as he could in the evolutionary push of the world towards the perfection which is the manifestation of the absolute, and this throughout his life was his ultimate concern: to bring each individual and the world into perfection as defined by *Vedānta*.[265]

265 Robert N. Minor, *Sarvepalli Radhakrishnan and Hinduism,* p. 322.

6

Conclusion

A comparative study of the religious ideas of four eminent contemporary Indian thinkers, namely, Raja Rammohun Roy, Swami Vivekananda, Mahatma Gandhi and Dr. Sarvepalli Radhakrishnan has been made in this work. Though their backgrounds are different but all of them belong to what is generally called as the period of Indian Renaissance.

All these thinkers have taken up the various issues in the philosophy of religion. They were not only well versed in the ancient lore of Hinduism, but also in the Western tradition and Christian thought. In their philosophical and religious ideas, we find a happy blend of all what is best in the Eastern and the Western traditions. They were the products of the Renaissance and at the same time they themselves contributed for the growth and progress of the spirit of Renaissance and much for the enrichment of contemporary Indian tradition. There are many similarities between them. On some issues they might have had some distinct opinions of their own. Yet all of them are theists and idealists, and had great appreciation for the ancient Indian tradition.

In general they have accepted the four paths of *karma*, *bhakti*, *jñāna* and *yoga* which lead to the realization of the ultimate reality. But some of them gave importance to one of them; for example, Raja Rammohun Roy gave importance to knowledge and devotion. Swami Vivekananda gave equal importance to all the four paths, but he felt that the path of *karma* was important. It is because of the need of enormous dynamism and action for the upliftment of India. Mahatma Gandhi gave importance to *bhakti* and *karma*. Though a man of devotion he spent his life with full of hectic activity and dynamism. Dr. Radhakrishnan gave importance to *Jñāna*, the path of knowledge, though he held equal preference for the other three.

Raja Rammohun Roy was influenced by *Vedānta* and *Upaniṣads*; Swami Vivekananda was also influenced by *Vedānta* but he was not much critical about popular Hinduism. Mahatma Gandhi gave importance mainly to *bhakti*. Radhakrishnan believed in the path of *Advaita Vedānta*. All these four thinkers, true to Indian tradition, were equally reverent to other traditions.

This ultimate aim of Indian philosophy and religion is the attainment of *mokṣa* (liberation). *Dharma, artha, kama* are called as *tri-vargas*. Through them one has to attain *mokṣa* which is called as *apavarga*. Except few thinkers like Jawaharlal Nehru and M.N. Roy, all other philosophers generally accept the concept of Moksha; and according to them, the highest aim of any individual should be the attainment of *mokṣa*.

Contemporary Indian philosophy is basically idealistic and is based on the philosophy of *Vedānta*. Though there are different interpretations on some of the concepts of *Vedānta*, all of them accepted the *Vedānta* tradition. Empiricism is not a popular philosophic system in India in the present times as well as in the past. The challenges of empiricism and materialism are there but not significant. Empiricism is equally an important and vital philosophic system; but it could not get a hold in contemporary Indian thought. There are many critics who consider that contemporary Indian religious thought is mainly interpretative but not creative. There is some truth. The contemporary Indian thinker is a defender of the tradition in the broad sense. He considers the scriptures to be sacred and valid and remarks that sometimes it is due to our incapacity that we are not in a position to understand the true meaning of scriptures.

It is wrong to think that the *Vedāntic* tradition is not creative like the method of the *Pūrvapakṣa* which doubts a particular judgement and tries to give an alternative answer. Through the system, questions are raised about a statement and attempts are made to give a reasonable answer. In contemporary Indian religious situation, there is no scope, at present, to place a new viewpoint, according to some scholars. If this argument is accepted, we have to say that contemporary religious thought tries to interpret the age-old tenets in the new light.

Another fact is that a discerning historian of religion finds that the new discoveries are made in science. If people are scientific and rational in their temperament and if they reject all that is irrational in our religions and belief system, they have to reject many tenets in many religions. But the modern man is using science where it is necessary with scientific temperament and when it comes to religion they give importance to faith than reason. If science is taken seriously and applied to religion, many of the major religions will loose many of their followers. But we find that science and faith are living together without a hindrance.

Some criticize the contemporary Indian thought as interpretative and not creative. These critics say that the contemporary Indian thinkers just wanted to interpret the *Vedāntic* scriptures to defend their views. Generally, these scriptures use verse language which gives scope for different interpretations whether it is *Quran* or *Bible* or *Bhagavad Gītā*. This gives scope for different schools of thought in every religion. In *Vedānta* also we have many schools like *Advaita*, *Viśiṣṭādvaita* or *Dvaita*, mainly propounded by Sankara, Ramanuja and Madhva based on the *Prasthāna-trayi—Brahma Sūtra*, *Upaniṣad*s and the *Gītā*. This flexibility of interpretation has its advantages and disadvantages. The advantage is that one can defend one's position by interpreting the verse in a way suitable to one. The disadvantage is that one might be blamed as instable and is not on a firm-ground.

Another problem is the question of what is truth? How can we know it? If we can know, is it through intellect or intuition? Is the intellect capable of knowing everything or are there any limitations to our intellectual or intuitional knowledge? Religious traditions give importance to intuition and consider it as one of the important sources of knowledge. How far the challenge of the empiricist is valid? In the history of many religious traditions, we find some men and women whom we call as mystics and *Ṛṣis*.

Importance of Religion

Though religion is given prominent place in every culture, its importance is paramount in Indian tradition. Whether one is a statesman or a social reformer, a patriot or an academician, one held religion in high esteem if he is a man of religion. Religion is a basis for any human endeavour in India whether it is literary, artistic, musical, social or political. The humanists like M.N. Roy and Jawaharlal Nehru tried to limit the role of religion. Modernization and industrialization also led to the limitation of the role of religion. Many sociologists considered that the role given to religion dwindles as the given society becomes more modernized. M.N. Roy who developed philosophy of Radical Humanism has given a naturalistic approach to the phenomena of religion.

Religion, Raja Rammohun Roy says, is a product of man's reason and the urge for freedom. He agreed with James Frazer that the age of religion was preceded by the age of magic. According to him, gods of natural religion arose to "rationalize the Barbarian, to explain the phenomena of nature and his experience thereof."[266] The gods of natural religion must be traced to one fundamental cause and thus arose the notion of the Almighty Creator.

266 M.N. Roy, *Religions, culture and Durga puja*, p. 26.

Roy maintained that the gods of natural religion and Supreme Being of monotheism were analogous to the hypotheses of science. Both science and religion attempt to explain the mysteries of nature, and religion was regarded by him as a background of science. He characterized religion as a "rational system of thought, limited by the inadequate stone of positive knowledge."[267]

He believed that the freedom of man is incompatible with the omnipotence of God; and therefore religious morality was condemned by him as spiritual terrorism. He wrote; "The religious man's morality is either hypocrisy or performed under duress. A materialist is moral by his own conviction. He practises virtue not as a payment for a place in heaven or for the salvation of his soul, but simply because he cannot help it."[268] In his ethical philosophy, Raja Rammohun Roy was essentially an epicurean. Both during his Marxist and humanist periods he attempted to reconcile ethics with rationalism and materialism in the philosophy of humanism.

Thus Marxist ideology and humanism in Raja Rammohun Roy go to the extent of relegating religion, and further to the limited roles. In the highly advanced Western society, functional value of religion has diminished. Jawaharlal Nehru, one of the builders of modern India, was also like M.N. Roy, who was influenced by socialism and humanism, gave importance to humanity than to religion. He considered humanity as his temple and service of fellowmen as his religion. In his opinion religion, as it is practised today all over the world, is an empty-shell having shed all its substance. No religion satisfied him fully, though he agreed with certain aspects of Hinduism in which he was born.

---

267 G.P. Bhattacharjee, *Evolution of political philosophy of M.N. Roy*, p. 121.

268 M.N. Roy, *Jail volumes* II, p. 123.

K.T.I. Narasimhachari points out that his views on renunciation underwent many changes; and he agrees with Einstein's statement that renunciation is the key to happiness. Einstein, the most eminent among scientists, tells us that the fate of the human race was more than ever dependent on its moral strength today. The way to a joyful and happy state is renunciation and self-limitation. Thus he takes us back suddenly from this proud period of science to the time of old philosophers, from the lust for power and the profit-motive to the spirit of renunciation with which India has been most familiar.

Many societies are becoming multi-religious. Due to globalization and migration on large scale, every society is becoming multi-religious and multi-ethnic. For example, the Christian nations like France, Germany, England and U.S.A are having good number of people of other religions as minorities. This multi-ethnic and multi-religious phenomenon leads to religious tolerance and secularism. In almost all democratic countries citizenship is not restricted to any particular religion. Similarly, language is also not the main criteria for getting citizenship. Thus a new type of political and social order is emerging in almost all the modern democracies.

In sociology and psychology, the phenomenon of religion is being studied from the point of scientific and functional basis. The sociologists and psychologists think that we need not deny the importance of religion but what is needed is the proper assessment of its role. As it is mentioned earlier, the Christian nations are becoming multi-religious and pluralistic because of mass-migration of other religious groups.[269] These philosophers, under study, are aware of the changes that have come up in Indian society. Their reflections on Indian society,

269 West Asia which was once predominately Muslim is having on rush of Hindus and Christians. Because of this changes, they are also slowly becoming secular.

to a great extent, are based on situations prevailing at that time. The problems they confronted and the solutions they offered are proper and appropriate in their context.

Ancient and Modern Philosophy

This is the way the modern philosophers are different from the ancient philosophers: Ancient philosophy generally conceives the tragic sense of life, and assumes the transcendental life as full of bliss and life in the world is not a boon but a curse. The traditional Indian religious thought is mainly salvation-oriented; and one must be on his own to attain his own salvation. Thus importance is given to individual salvation, except the Buddha. But the contemporary thinkers stressed on group salvation—the salvation of the humanity. The modern Indian thinkers gave importance to collective salvation.

Another important aspect of the contemporary philosophy is about the changes in the concepts of empirical and existential man, which has given precedence over the non-qualifiable soul. The soul is replaced by man and God is replaced by society; and the other world is replaced by humanity. Thus, some traditional concepts got new meanings and contents. The contemporary Indian religious thought gave equal importance to both the spiritual values and worldly problems; and we find the blend of these two—that of spiritual and material. As Prof. B.K. Lal rightly points out:

> "Philosophy in India invariably arises in some such acts of meditative speculation. It was so with the *Vedic* seer and also with the *Upaniṣadic* thinker; and it continues to be so even with the contemporary Indian thinker."[270]

Generally, it is considered that experience is the basis of Western philosophy. But meditative speculation has been the method of the Indian philosopher. Through meditative insight, the Indian philosopher wants to find a rational justification for his

---

270 B.K. Lal, *Contemporary Indian philosophy*, p. IV.

traditional doctrines. Indian tradition believes that truth can be known only through supra-rational cognition. Another important difference between ancient and modern philosophy is the concept of soul. Modern philosophers wanted to study the predicament of man instead of trying to study the elusive nature of soul. Thus the developed behavioural sciences had their impact on the modern philosophers—both in the East and the West. Contemporary Indian philosophers are also influenced by these developments.

The doctrines of *karma,* immortality, sin, salvation, rebirth, etc. are the age-old problems. The contemporary Indian thinkers discussed about these in the light of rationalism and science. These problems are still relevant. They also discussed about the psychological problems like the stages of consciousness. They took the help of modern psychology to understand some of the psychological concepts which were discussed in philosophy. The problem of suffering is an important concept in Indian philosophy. For Buddhism, it is the main issue. The modern philosophers also want to know the psychological, political, social and other causes of suffering.

We can find agreement between the traditional and contemporary thinkers on some of the issues like monism, reality of the world, integral nature of man, reality of human freedom and importance of intuitive knowledge. Most of them were highly critical of some social customs of Hindu society, which they considered as irrelevant.

Regarding non-violence, the prominent value in Indian tradition, all these thinkers consider it should be accepted without any reservation. But Sri Aurobindo accepts violence as a part of divine scheme. In this context, his perspective is nearer to the *Gītā*'s ideal of action for *dharma*. As per Hindu tradition, the concept of trinity i.e., Brahma, *Viṣṇu* and *Maheśvara* represents three principles of creation, sustenance and destruction or punishment. Similarly, the *Gita* says that evil doers must be punished.

The early *Vadāntic* thinkers had confrontation with Buddhism and Jainism, which contain different doctrines challenging the *Vedānta* philosophy. Similarly, in the contemporary times, three doctrines challenged the *Vedānta* philosophy. They are Christianity, Islam and Marxism. The doctrines of these religions are a great challenge to *Vedānta* philosophy.

To the traditional Indian thinkers, war and violence were never the major issues. They considered that there was nothing wrong in waging war against evil-doers and annexing a country. But today war has a global relevance; and man's concern is international peace. Due to nuclear proliferation and the devastating effects of the expected nuclear-war, the international community wants to solve their problems through peaceful means. Ideological conflicts should be avoided and there should be scope for dialogue between conflicting nations.

The contemporary Indian thinkers consider that problems can be solved through religion. For them, any one who can understand religion can strive for harmony and peace. They also consider that the intellectual knowledge has limitations. Immanuel Kant and Bergson also held the same opinion. Contemporary Indian thinkers wanted reformation and change in the Indian society. In the traditional thought, the concept of *Puruṣārthas—Dharma, artha, kāma* and *mokṣa*—was given importance. A householder is expected to give importance to all the four *Puruṣārthas*. The modern Indian thinkers have accepted this concept and considered that we should give equal importance to worldly life as well as the spiritual life.

Modern Indian thinkers have great respect not only for religion but also for humanity. Most of them had their education in schools, where Christian religious principles were strictly observed. They had a thorough knowledge of the *Holy Bible* and the Christianity. Thus they have positive attitude towards Christianity. They also believe that God is one, whether one calls him as Christ, Allah or Kṛṣṇa. They firmly believe that different religions are different ways to reach salvation. They also consider that it is not possible to have one universal religion. Even if we try to eliminate all religions and keep one in due course; that religion will also become many. It is a fact that, even the religions like Christianity and Islam, those believe in one scripture, *Bible or Quran,* have been divided into a number of denominations. So the Indian thinkers believe in plurality of religions.

The modern ideologies like humanism, secularism and socialism are dominant; and they have become universal ideologies almost. For them, no one can be critical of their doctrines. To them secularism means not isolation of religion from political and civic life but tolerance of other religions. Their socialism is not simply materialistic but spiritual. *Vedāntic* socialism is different from Marxian socialism. It does not believe in class struggle and material explanation of nature, world and man. It believed in the spiritual nature of man and in his intrinsic goodness. Their humanism is also based on spiritualism; however they cannot accept that man can shape his own destiny without the intervention of God. Thus their view is theistic and their humanism may be considered as religious humanism.

According to these thinkers, science has a limited role; they considered that there cannot be any conflict between science and true religion. Their religion is not simply the Hindu religion, but they believed in 'Universal Religion'. They considered that everyone could follow one's own religion and at the same time extend respect for other religions. This respect for other religions is not based on mere courtesy and good manners, but it springs from the belief that every religion is equally true.

Generally in philosophy, every thinker wants to build a system out of his ideas. It is felt that everyone must build a system to be called a philosopher. But system building has its own perils. In system building, we find concepts which are necessary to strengthen a system, so they are conveniently brought in thought that does not suit to it. All these philosophers are aware of the challenges that come from modern ideologies based on atheism and existentialism.

The ancient philosophers approached life with a tragic sense. They considered that the life was full of suffering and the aim of religion and philosophy was to find the ways and means to attain freedom from suffering. This problem is tackled in a different way by the modern thinkers. So they accept the reality of suffering and consider the possibility of an escape from it. Some consider that suffering is a part of life and it should be faced with fortitude and dignity.

Philosophy is concerned not only with the individual but also with the society. The ancient Indian philosophers think that complete control of the body, the senses and the mind is essential for spiritual growth. The world is considered as the only field for action. The body is considered as the temple of the divine:

> "It is by emphasizing the reality of these and by assigning to the body and the senses some role in the process of spiritual growth that the contemporary Indian thinkers consider themselves to be close to the empirical and the matter-of-fact attitude of the present times."[271]

In Indian tradition, philosophy is defined as *darśana* or vision. Thus, philosophy is practical and can solve the problems. The ancient Indian philosophers also considered that suffering was due to the ignorance with reference to the nature of the real. When we are not in a position to know the difference between *sat* (real) and the *asat* (unreal), we develop attachment for the unreal; and thus we suffer.

---

271 B.K. Lal, *Contemporary Indian philosophy*, p. XV.

Salvation is an important concept in Indian philosophy. It is called as *mukti, mokṣa,* or *Nirvāṇa*. Thus, we have different names for the state of bliss. The concept of bliss also differs from one system to the other. Similarly, some of the concepts like *anubhava* (experience), which was discussed in *Vedānta,* are finding new interpretations through modern psychology. The problems are perennial and always existing. Man wants to know about himself and his relation with the world and with other fellow beings and about his relation with the ultimate reality. Man can find some answers to these issues. Thus man continues to search for answers to the problems.

According to some ancient thinkers, the world is real and for others it is not real. But the modern philosophers accept the empirical reality of the world. Similarly, regarding intuition and intellect the classical philosophers gave importance to intuition, whereas the contemporary philosophers gave equal importance to both intellect and intuition. In the traditional philosophy, the concept of freedom and individual dignity were not well conceived. But the contemporary philosophers due to the impact of Western liberal, political and social ideas and due to the development of philosophies like humanism, began to give due importance to the concept of freedom and human dignity.

As earlier philosophies were developed before pre-industrial era, the issues like equality, dignity of labour, equal distribution of wealth, equality before law, the concept of social justice and other concepts were not known. Similarly, the philosophical problems that emerged out of war, violence and nuclear proliferation were not the issues for the classical philosophers.

But the socio-economic development of the present century is throwing up new challenges. Similarly, regarding religion the early societies were habituated to live in mono-religious societies. But now, every advanced country is multi-religious and multi-ethnic. This situation leads us to develop new ideas regarding tolerance and harmony. Thus we find the contemporary Indian philosophers are faced with new problems which are the products of industrialization, modernization and globalization. They want to apply modern and scientific methods in the philosophical field to find solutions to these problems. Regarding certain basic concepts, we find almost unanimity in these thinkers.

Regarding the system of *Vedānta*, contemporary Indian philosophers consider that it is value-oriented and has universal appeal. As we have seen earlier even in *Vedānta* we find different interpretations, but the core concepts are almost the same. In *Vedānta, Brahman* is considered as supreme reality; and all these thinkers accepted the same, though we find some differences among these thinkers. All these thinkers were the products of the Indian Renaissance; and as such they have belief that India again can become a rich and prosperous country when its civilization and culture is revived. They also felt that India can play a vital role in the international arena.

The contemporary Indian philosophers were theists; and they considered that all people could not reach the higher level of worshiping the *Nirguṇa Brahman*. So the individual has to choose a path, which is suitable to his temperament. Regarding religion and its efficacy, they held high opinion. They felt that human activities, whether it was political, economic or social should be permeated with the spirit of religion. They believed that religion should not make one dogmatic. It should make liberal, humane and moral. When the true spirit of religion is imbibed there is no scope for violence and hatred. Ethical values based on humanism are acceptable but at one stage there is a need for religion. They consider that Indian civilization and culture is based on the bedrock of religion. Once religion becomes irrelevant, India looses its greatness and glory.

It is interesting to note that all the advanced countries are trying to build their future on the basis of rationalism, humanism and secularism. The contemporary Indian thinkers, while appreciating and accepting the role of the values of rationalism, humanism and secularism, asserted that religion should be relegated to the background. They considered that religion and the values of rationalism, humanism and secularism could go together. National progress should not hinder the spirit of true religion.

All these thinkers believed in religious pluralism and considered that the true essence of all religions was the same. As such everyone should be allowed to follow one's own religion. Most of them felt that no religion should encourage conversions. It is their belief that all religions are equally true. They considered that every citizen should have respect for other religions and try to know about other religions to imbibe their spirit.

Regarding certain practices and beliefs of Hinduism, they have certain divergences. For example, Raja Rammohun Roy considered that idol worship was wrong. He expressed the view that the *Brahman* should be worshiped and for the worship of the Absolute it is not necessary to have idols. But other thinkers were not against it. For example, Vivekananda, Mahatma Gandhi and Radhakrishnan considered that the ordinary people could not worship the ultimate, *Nirguṇa Brahman*, God without qualities. Raja Rammohun Roy also rejected the doctrine of incarnation (*avatāra*) while others accepted it. They felt the need of blending religion and science, and gave importance to the development of science and technology. They gave importance to work and worship, and believed that only through hard work and industry India could become prosperous.

Regarding universal religion, they have two opinions, for example, Raja Rammohun Roy, and to some extent Swami Vivekananda, considered that *Vedānta* had the possibility of becoming a universal religion. Radhakrishnan also supported this viewpoint to some extent. The other opinion is that all religions are equally efficacious; and what is needed is not universal religion but inter-religious understanding and appreciation. Even if we make all people follow the religion of *Vedānta*, in due course it will proliferate into different religions. It is because of the fact that the human spirit always cherishes alternatives, divergences and plurality.

All civilizations, cultures and ethnic groups are not at the same stage of development. Hence, they need different religions and different types of worship to suit their social and cultural needs. All these thinkers supported this viewpoint and considered that there should be scope for unity and diversity.

Bibliography

Anna. *Saints of India.* Madras: Sri Ramakrishna Math, 1966.

Antoine, Robert. *Religious Hinduism: a presentation and appraisal.* Bombay: St. Paul Publications, 1966.

Arnold, Matthew. *Literature and dogma: an essay towards a better apprehension of the Bible.* New York: Macmillan and Co., 1926.

Arunachalam, M. *Cultural heritage of Hinduism.* Tiruppanandal: The Kasi Math, 1982.

Awasthi, Brahma Mitra. *Divine path by holy saints.* Delhi: Swami Keshawananda Yoga Institute, 1985.

Bahm, Archie J. *The world's living religions.* New Delhi: Arnold Heineman, 1977.

Baird, Robert D. *Religion in modern India.* New Delhi: Manohar, 1981.

Balasubramanian, R, and T.S. Devadoss. *Gandhian thought.* Madras: University of Madras, 1981.

Bali, Dev Raj. *Modern Indian thought: Rammohan Roy to Jayaprakash Narayan.* New Delhi: Sterling Publishers Private Ltd., 1980.

Bandyopadhyay, Pranab. *Swami Vivekananda and the modern world.* Calcutta: United Writers, 1990.

Banerjee, Nikunja Vihari. *The future of religion.* New Delhi: Munshiram Manoharlal, 1981.

Banhatti, G S. *The life and philosophy of Swami Vivekananda.* New Delhi: Atlantic Publishers & Distributors, 1995.

Barrett, William, and Henry David Aiken. *Philosophy in the twentieth century, an anthology.* New York: Random House, 1962.

Barth, Auguste. *The religions of India.* Delhi: S. Chand, 1980.

Besant, Annie Wood. *Four great religions: four lectures.* London: Theosophical Pub. Society, 1897.

Bhattacharyya, Haridas. *The cultural heritage of India.* Calcutta: Ramakrishna Mission, Institute of Culture, 1953.

Bhattacharyya, Krishnachandra. *Studies in Vedantism.* Calcutta: Calcutta University, 1963.

Bondurant, Joan V. *Conquest of violence; the Gandhian philosophy of conflict.* Princeton: Princeton University Press, 1958.

Bose, Nirmal Kumar. *Selections from Gandhi.* Ahmedabad: Navajivan Pub. House, 1948.

Bouquet, A. C. *Hinduism.* London: Hutchinson University Library, 1948.

Brightman, A. *Philosophy of religion.* New Jersey: Prentice Hall, 1956.

Budhananda, Swami. *The saving challenge of religion.* Madras: Sri Ramakrishna Math, 1980.

Burke, Marie Louise. *Swami Vivekananda: his second visit to the West, new discoveries.* Calcutta: Advaita Ashrama, 1973.

—. *Swami Vivekanda in America.* Calcutta: Advaita Ashrama, 1971.

Canney, Maurice Arthur. *An encyclopedia of religions.* Delhi: Nag Publishers, 1976.

Chakravarthy, Amiya. *Modern Hinduism.* Madras: University of Madras, 1968.

Chatterjee, R.K. *The Gita and its culture.* London: Oriental University Press, 1987.

Chatterjee, Satischandra. *Classical Indian philosophies: their synthesis in the philosophy of Sri Ramakrishna.* Calcutta: University of Calcutta, 1963.

Chattopadhyaya, Rajagopal. *Swami Vivekananda in India: a corrective biography.* Delhi: Motilal Banarsidass Publishers, 1999.

Chaturvedi, Laxmi Narayan. *The teachings of Bhagavad Gita.* New Delhi: Sterling Publishers, 1991.

Damodaran, K. *Indian thought: a critical survey.* Bombay: Asia Pub. House, 1967.

Das, Bhagavan. *The essential unity of all religions.* Delhi: Munshiram Manoharlal, 1964.

Datta, D. K. *Social, moral and religious philosophy of Mahatma Gandhi.* New Delhi: Intellectual Publishing House, 1980.

Desai, Makhadev Haribhai. *The gospel of selfless action: or the Gita, according to Gandhi.* Ahmedabad: Navajivan Pub. House, 1951.

Diwakar, Ranganath Ramachandra. *Gandhi, the spiritual seeker.* Bombay: Bharatiya Vidya Bhavan, 1964.

Earhart Byran, H. *Religious traditions of the world.* USA: Harper Collins Publishers, 1933.

Edwards, D.M. *The philosophy of religion.* London: Hutchinson Publishing House, 1966.

Edwards, Rem Blanchard. *Reason and religion: an introduction to the philosophy of religion.* New York: Harcourt Brace Jovanovich, 1972.

Farquhar, J.N., and Griswold, H.D. *The religious quest of India.* London: Oxford University Press, 1920.

Fischer, Louis. *Gandhi: his life and message for the world.* New York: Signet Key Books, 1954.

Gandhi, M.K. *My religion.* Ahmedabad: Navajivan Publishing House, 1977.

—. *Non-violence in peace & war.* Ahmedabad: Navajivan Publishing House, 1960-1962.

—. *Non–Violence.* Ahmedabad: Navajivan Publishing House, 1954.

—. *All religions are true.* Bombay: Bharatiya Vidya Bhavan, 1957.

—. *Communal unity.* Ahmedabad: Navajivan Pub. House, 1949.

—. *Ethical religion.* Ahmedabad: Navajivan Pub. House, 1968.

—. *Hindu dharma.* Ahmedabad: Navajivan Pub. House, 1950.

—. *In search of the Supreme.* Ahmedabad: Navajivan Pub. House, 1961.

—. *Sarvodaya.* Ahmedabad: Navajivan Pub. House, 1954.

—. *Satyagraha.* Ahmedabad: Navajivan Pub. House, 1951.

—. *The story of my experiments with truth.* Ahmedabad: Navajivan Press, 1959.

—. *The voice of truth.* Ahmedabad: Navajivan Pub. House, 1969.

—. *Women and social injustice.* Ahmedabad: Navajivan Pub. House, 1942.

Ganguly, Mano Mohan. *The Swami Vivekananda: a study.* Calcutta: Contemporary Publishers, 1962.

George, Galloway. *The philosophy of religions.* Edinburgh: International Theological Library, 1925.

Ghanananda, Swami, and Edward Geoffrey Parrinder. *Swami Vivekananda in East and West.* London: The Ramakrishna Vedanta Centre, 1968.

Griswold, Harvey De. Witt. *The religion of the Rigveda.* London: Oxford University, 1923.

Hastings, James. *Encyclopedia of religion and ethics.* New York, Edinburgh, 1971.

Hick, John. *Philosophy of religion.* New Delhi: Prentice-Hall of India, 1978.

Hill, W. D.P. *The Bhagavad Gita.* London: Oxford University Press, 1928.

Hopkins, R.W. *Origin and evolution of religion.* Delhi: Bharatiya Vidya Prakashan, 1987.

Husain, S. Abid. *The national culture of India.* New Delhi: National Book Trust, 1978.

Isherwood, Christopher. *Vedanta for the modern man.* New York: Harper and Bross, 1957.

Iyer, M.K.V. *Advaita vedanta according to Sankara.* New York, 1964.

Joshi, V.C. *Rammohun Roy and the process of modernization in India.* Delhi: Vikas Pub. House, 1975.

Jung, C.G. *Modern man in search of a soul.* New York: Harcourt, Brace, 1933.

Kar, Bijayananda. *Indian philosophy: an analytical study*. Delhi: Ajanta Publications, 1985.

Kripalani, J.B. *Gandhian thought*. Chandigarh: Panjab University Publication Bureau, 1964.

Lal, Basant Kumar. *Contemporary Indian philosophy*. Delhi: Motilal Banarsidass, 1978.

Lal, Rajendra Behari. *Religion in the light of reason and science*. Bombay: Bharatiya Vidya Bhavan, 1978.

MacDermott, Robert A. *Basic writings of S. Radhakrishnan*. Bombay: Jaico Publishing House, 1970.

Mahadevan, Telliyavaram Mahadevan Ponnambalam. *Swami Vivekananda and the Indian renaissance*. Coimbatore: Sri Ramakrishna Mission Vidyalaya Teachers College, 1967.

Minor, Robert N. *Radhakrishnan: a religious biography*. Albany: State Univ. of New York Pr., 1987.

Muller, Max F. *Ram Mohan to Ramakrishna*. Calcutta, 1952.

Murty, K. Satchidananda. *The Indian spirit*. Waltair: Andhra University Press, 1965.

—. *Indian philosophy since 1498*. Visakhapatnam: Andhra University, 1982.

Muttu Cumraru, T. *Vivekananda, prophet of the new age of India and world*. Cylone: The Ramakrishna Mission, 1963.

Nanda, B.R. *Mahatma Gandhi: a biography*. London: Allen & Unwin, 1958.

Naravane, Vishwanath S. *Modern Indian thought*. New Delhi: Orient Longman, 1978.

Prabhu, R.K. and U.R. Rao. *The mind of Mahatma Gandhi*. Ahmedabad: Navajivan Publishing House, 1969.

Radhakrishnan, S. *Eastern religion and Western thought*. London: Oxford University Press, 1940.

—. *Glimpses of world religions*. Bombay: Jaico Pub. House, 1958.

—. *Indian philosophy*. London: Allen & Unwin, 1941.

—. *Religion and society.* London: Allen & Unwin, 1956.

—. *Religion in a changing world.* London: Allen & Unwin, 1967.

—. *The Hindu view of life: Upton lectures delivered at Manchester college,* Oxford, 1926. London: George Allen & Unwin, 1948.

—. *The principal Upanishads.* New Delhi: Indus, 1994.

—. *The religion we need.* Varanasi: Banaras Hindu University Press, 1963.

—. *An idealist view of life.* London: George Allen & Unwin, 1951.

—. *The Bhagavad-Gita.* London: George Allen &Unwin, 1948.

Radhakrishnan, Sarvepalli. *Religion and culture.* Delhi: Orient Paperbacks, 1987.

—. *The Brahma Sutra, the philosophy of spiritual life.* London: G. Allen and Unwin, 1960.

Richards, Glyn. *A source-book of modern Hinduism.* London: Curzon Press, 1996.

Sarma, D. S. *Studies in the renaissance of Hinduism in the nineteenth and twentieth centuries.* Benares: Benares Hindu University, 1944.

—. *Hinduism through the ages.* Bombay: Bharatiya Vidya Bhavan, 1962.

Saroja, G. V. *Contemporary Indian philosophy.* New Delhi: Sterling, 1985.

Schilpp, Paul Arthur. *The philosophy of Sarvepalli Radhakrishnan.* Delhi: Motilal Banarsidass, 1992.

Sharma, Arvind. *Ramakrishna and Vivekananda: new perspectives.* New Delhi: Sterling Publishers, 1989.

Sharma, Nilima. *Twentieth century Indian philosophy: nature and destiny of man.* Varanasi: Bharatiya Vidya Prakasana, 1972.

Shastri, Ram Dev. *Glimpses of world religions: basic tenets & philosophy.* Bombay: Jaico Pub. House, 1957.

Shukla, Chandrashanker. *Gandhi's view of life.* Bombay: Bharatiya Vidya Bhavan, 1960.

Sinha, Raghuvir. *Social change in Indian society.* Delhi: Concept Pub. Co, 1978.

Venkatesananda, Swami. *Enlightened living: A new interpretative translation of the Yoga Sutra of Maharsi Patanjali.* Delhi: Motilal Barnarsidass, 1978.

Vidyatmananda. *What religion is: In the words of Swami Vivekananda.* Calcutta: Advaita Ashrama, 1972.

Vivekananda Swami. *Raja yoga.* Calcutta: Advaita Ashrama, 1980.

—. *Bhakti yoga.* Calcutta: Advaita Ashrama, 1978.

—. *Jnana yoga.* Calcutta: Advaita Ashrama, 1980.

—. *Raja yoga or conquering the internal nature.* Calcutta: Advaita Ashrama, 1973.

—. *The nationalists and religious lectures of Swami Vivekananda.* Calcutta: Advaita Ashrama, 1998.

—. *Chicago addresses.* Calcutta: Advaita Ashrama, 1958.

—. *Letters of Swami Vivekananda.* Calcutta: Advaita Ashrama, 1993.

—. *Selections from Swami Vivekananda.* Calcutta: Advaita Ashrama, 1963.

—. *Selections from the complete works of Swami Vivekananda.* Calcutta: Advaita Ashrama, 2000.

—. *The complete works of Swami Vivekananda.* Calcutta: Advaita Ashrama, 1989.

—. *Vivekananda sahitya sancayana.* Nagpur: Ramkrishna Math, 1988.

Walker, Benjamin. *Hindu world: An encyclopedic survey of Hinduism.* London: Allen & Unwin, 1968.

Index

J

K

L

M

T